Development Redefined

Titles in the Series

The Rules of the Game: A Primer on International Relations, by Mark R. Amstutz

Development Redefined: How the Market Met Its Match, by Robin Broad and John Cavanagh

A Tale of Two Quagmires: Iraq, Vietnam, and the Hard Lessons of War, by Kenneth J. Campbell

Celebrity Diplomacy, by Andrew F. Cooper

People Count! Networked Individuals in Global Politics, by James N. Rosenau

Paradoxes of Power: U.S. Foreign Policy in a Changing World, edited by David Skidmore

Global Democracy and the World Social Forums, by Jackie Smith and Marina Karides, et al.

Forthcoming

Sixteen Million One: Understanding Civil War, by Patrick M. Regan

Spirits Talking: Six Conversations on Right and Wrong in the Affairs of States, by Stephen D. Wrage

Development Redefined

How the Market Met Its Match

Robin Broad and John Cavanagh

Paradigm Publishers
Boulder • London

Published in the United States by Paradigm Publishers, 3360 Mitchell Lane, Suite E, Boulder, Colorado 80301 USA.

Paradigm Publishers is the trade name of Birkenkamp & Company, LLC, Dean Birkenkamp, President and Publisher.

Library of Congress Cataloging-in-Publication Data

Broad, Robin.
    Development redefined : how the market met its match / by Robin Broad,
John Cavanagh.
        p. cm. — (International studies intensives)
    Includes bibliographic references and index.
    ISBN 978-1-59451-522-4 (hbk. : alk. paper)
    ISBN 978-1-59451-523-1 (pbk. : alk. paper)
    1. Economic development—Developing countries.   2. Globalization—Economic aspects.   3. International economic relations.   I. Cavanagh, John, 1955–   II. Title.
    HC59.7.B68846 2008
    338.9009172'4—dc22

                                                                                    2008011268

Printed and bound in the United States of America on acid-free paper that meets the standards of the American National Standard for Permanence of Paper for Printed Library Materials.

Designed and Typeset by Straight Creek Bookmakers.

13   12   11   10   09   1   2   3   4   5

In memory of
Dick Barnet, James Chace, and Bill Maynes—
who launched us as writers,
and whose wise counsel and contagious laughter we miss dearly.

Contents

Development Redefined: A Time Line *ix*

1 What Is Development? 1

2 The Washington Consensus Emerges 13

3 The Citizen Backlash Erupts (with Walden Bello) 27

4 Myths About the Environment Strengthen 41

5 The North-South Divide Widens 53

6 The Washington Consensus Cracks 67

7 Post-9/11: Myths About Aid and Trade Resurface 79

8 New Lenses on Development 91

Notes *109*

Acknowledgments *125*

Index *127*

About the Authors *139*

Development Redefined
A Time Line

Washington Consensus and Elite Time Line		**Alter-Globalization Movement Time Line**

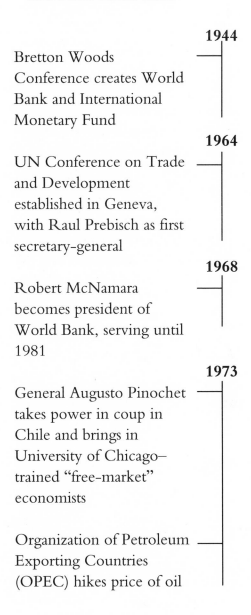

1944

Bretton Woods Conference creates World Bank and International Monetary Fund

1964

UN Conference on Trade and Development established in Geneva, with Raul Prebisch as first secretary-general

1968

Robert McNamara becomes president of World Bank, serving until 1981

1973

General Augusto Pinochet takes power in coup in Chile and brings in University of Chicago–trained "free-market" economists

Organization of Petroleum Exporting Countries (OPEC) hikes price of oil

1974

UN General Assembly
adopts Declaration on the
New International
Economic Order

IMF creates extended fund
facilities (EFFs)

1975

Indigenous communities in
the northern Philippines
send letter to World Bank
president McNamara, asking
the Bank to stop funding the
Chico Dam

1978

China initiates market-
opening reforms

1979

Margaret Thatcher elected
prime minister of the
United Kingdom; serves
until 1990

OPEC carries out second
round of oil price hikes

1980

World Bank approves first structural adjustment loans (SALs), including one to the Philippines

Over the 1980s, environmental movements grow in Taiwan, protesting damage caused by export-led growth

1981

Ronald Reagan elected president of the United States, serving until 1989

1982

Mexico announces inability to service its external debt, signaling the onset of the debt crisis

Helmut Kohl elected chancellor of Germany, serving until 1998

1984

Workers rights' advocates convince U.S. Congress to amend Generalized System of Preferences (GSP) to deny trade benefits to countries violating worker rights

1985

U.S. treasury secretary
James Baker puts forth
"Baker Plan" for Third
World debt

World Bank gives loan to
India for Narmada Dam, as
large-scale protests against
the dam spread across India
and around the world

1986

"People Power" overthrows
Marcos dictatorship in
Philippines

Citizen groups begin annual
gatherings and protests at
World Bank and IMF
meetings

1987

Labor unrest breaks out in
South Korea

1989

U.S.-Canada free-trade
agreement comes into effect

"Anti-IMF" riots in
Venezuela; 300 people killed

Fall of the Berlin Wall sym-
bolizes end of the Cold War

1990

John Williamson details
the term "Washington
Consensus" in an Institute
for International
Economics publication

Citizen groups in Mexico,
Canada, and United States
unite to oppose NAFTA and
offer alternatives

1992

UN Conference on Environment and Development ("Earth Summit") held in Rio de Janeiro, Brazil

Levi Strauss and Co. passes first voluntary corporate code of conduct

1994

North American Free Trade Agreement (NAFTA) enters into force

Mayan peasants launch Zapatista uprising in southern Mexico

International Forum on Globalization established as global network of researchers and activists

Free Trade Area of the Americas (FTAA) negotiations begin

1995

World Trade Organization (WTO) opens its doors, subsuming the General Agreement on Tariffs and Trade (GATT)

James Wolfensohn selected president of the World Bank, serving until 2005

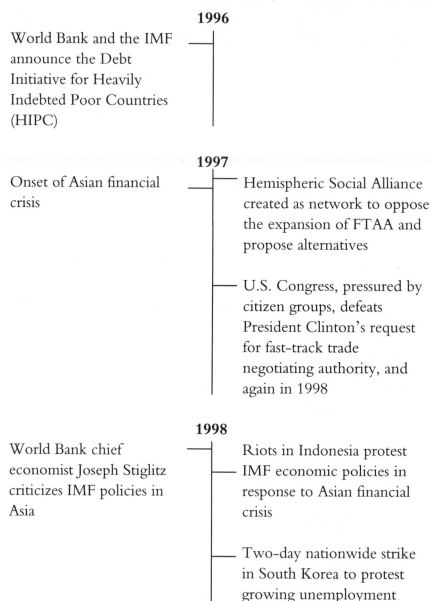

1996

World Bank and the IMF
announce the Debt
Initiative for Heavily
Indebted Poor Countries
(HIPC)

1997

Onset of Asian financial
crisis

Hemispheric Social Alliance
created as network to oppose
the expansion of FTAA and
propose alternatives

U.S. Congress, pressured by
citizen groups, defeats
President Clinton's request
for fast-track trade
negotiating authority, and
again in 1998

1998

World Bank chief
economist Joseph Stiglitz
criticizes IMF policies in
Asia

Riots in Indonesia protest
IMF economic policies in
response to Asian financial
crisis

Two-day nationwide strike
in South Korea to protest
growing unemployment

Asian financial crisis
spreads to Russia, and then
Latin America

U.S. Congress establishes
Meltzer Commission to
examine role of the
international financial
institutions

Citizen coalitions in several
countries stop proposed
Multilateral Agreement on
Investment

Hugo Chavez elected
president of Venezuela

1999

60,000 activists help shut
down WTO negotiations in
"Battle of Seattle"

2000

Governments gather at
United Nations to
announce Millennium
Development Goals to cut
extreme poverty in half by
the year 2015

Massive protests against IMF
and World Bank in
Washington and Prague

2001

First World Social Forum
held in Porto Alegre, Brazil,
as citizens' alternative to
annual Davos World
Economic Forum

Large-scale protests against
FTAA at Summit of the
Americas in Quebec City

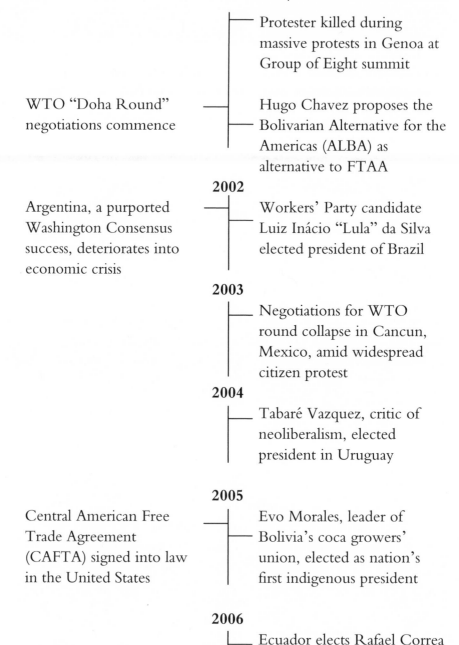

Protester killed during
massive protests in Genoa at
Group of Eight summit

WTO "Doha Round"
negotiations commence

Hugo Chavez proposes the
Bolivarian Alternative for the
Americas (ALBA) as
alternative to FTAA

2002

Argentina, a purported
Washington Consensus
success, deteriorates into
economic crisis

Workers' Party candidate
Luiz Inácio "Lula" da Silva
elected president of Brazil

2003

Negotiations for WTO
round collapse in Cancun,
Mexico, amid widespread
citizen protest

2004

Tabaré Vazquez, critic of
neoliberalism, elected
president in Uruguay

2005

Central American Free
Trade Agreement
(CAFTA) signed into law
in the United States

Evo Morales, leader of
Bolivia's coca growers'
union, elected as nation's
first indigenous president

2006

Ecuador elects Rafael Correa
on a campaign of prioritizing
the poor

2007

Hugo Chavez announces that Venezuela will withdraw from World Bank and IMF and create an alternative Banco del Sur

World Bank president Paul Wolfowitz resigns after ethics scandal

Bolivia withdraws from World Bank's International Center for the Settlements of Investment Disputes (ICSID)

Former U.S. trade representative Robert Zoellick selected by U.S. government as World Bank president

Ecuador announces willingness to leave 20 percent of its oil in the ground in exchange for debt cancellation and aid

Dominique Strauss-Kahn selected by Europeans as IMF managing director

Seven Latin American governments launch Banco del Sur

Citizen groups rally behind slogan of "global climate justice" at intergovernmental negotiations on climate in Bali, Indonesia

Chapter 1

What Is Development?

Abraham—subsistence farmer, community organizer, member of an indigenous community—forms his words slowly and deliberately: "Why is it that rich countries give aid, investments, and trade that are supposed to help us, but that end up destroying us? If you really want to help us, go back to your country and figure out why the world works this way."

It is the late 1970s in the southern Philippines. Robin has been living with Abraham's family in the province of Bukidnon, a land of mountains and forests and of ancient varieties of corn and rice where indigenous communities till land farmed by their ancestors for generations. Robin's sojourn comes at a moment of intense struggle over control of those ancestral lands: Transnational agribusiness firms are expanding their plantations of pineapple for export, Philippine elites are using political connections with dictator Ferdinand Marcos to gain land titles to grow sugar for the world market, and international aid agencies are drawing up plans to dam the river.

Robin returns to live in the Philippines in the early 1980s, as World Bank technocrats push policies to accelerate further the shift to export agriculture and manufacturing all over the country so that ordinary people like Abraham can become more "productive." Thousands are losing their lands in the name of "development."

Decades later, the two of us visit Abraham's family together. But the indigenous community is no more. Some of the land has been flooded by the dams. The pineapple plantations stretch as far as the eye can see, jutting

1

up against vast sugar plantations. The forests are distant memories. In Manila, we are told by government officials that the economy of the southern Philippines is growing, but what we see and hear when we visit Abraham's family is that the majority of people and the forests that sustained them are not. People who were poor but subsisting when Robin lived with them in the late 1970s now seem desperate.

This book is an attempt to understand what happened in communities like Abraham's. It is an attempt to answer Abraham's question after thirty years of inquiry. Now is the right moment to do so: We are nearly a decade into the new century, at a moment that marks the end of what may well be the most destructive development era of modern history. This book travels back in time, deep into that era, and then moves forward to examine the possibilities for a better future.

Throughout, the book revolves around the key questions inherent in Abraham's challenge to Robin three decades ago: What is "development"? Development for whom and by whom? How does one make it happen? Is "development" necessarily positive? What happens when external forces, beyond the control of local communities, become the determining factors and when development is defined narrowly as economic growth?[1]

Nearly three decades ago, elite institutions and individuals announced that the quest to find the answers to these questions had ended. The truths of development had been uncovered: Development was economic growth. And the magic button for catalyzing economic growth was clear: Let the invisible hand of the free-market reign. This orthodoxy placed free markets on a pedestal and asserted that unfettered private sectors are better than governments in solving the world's economic woes. Moreover, it was said that resolving such economic woes through economic growth would automatically translate into resolving social, political, and environmental woes. The answer was presented as fact—as undisputable fact proven by economic theory. There was to be no more debate.

There are few precedents in history to the drastic shift in global economic orthodoxy that occurred in the half-decade between 1980 and 1985. After two decades (1960 to 1980) of countries pursuing vastly different development paths, many of them successful in raising standards of living, dozens of countries pursued a radical shift in policy over the course of a mere half-decade.

And thus started the reign of what became known as the "Washington Consensus," or "neoliberalism," or what financier George Soros aptly termed "market fundamentalism"[2] in the 1980s and 1990s. It was economist John Williamson (then of the Washington, D.C.–based Institute for International Economics) who coined the phrase "Washington Consensus" to sum up this growing policy consensus in ten areas of economic reform that reflected free-market strategies to achieve export-led growth—with specific policies ranging from trade liberalization to privatization of state-owned firms.[3] The Washington Consensus, he argued, was shared by "both the political Washington of Congress and senior members of the administration, and the technocratic Washington of the international financial institutions, the economic agencies of the U.S. government, the Federal Reserve Board, and the think tanks."[4]

"Washington Consensus"—it is a curious but fitting term. And we cannot help but comment on its even more curious—and biased—research design: Polling such D.C.-based elites as those at the World Bank, the IMF, and the U.S. government in the late 1980s for views on development is akin to polling those in power at the Ministry of Magic and the Death Eaters AFTER the Dark Lord has taken control to determine the prevailing consensus and to intimate that the new elite consensus reflects the "correct" way forward. Should not the researcher poll Harry Potter and his followers?

Indeed, the Washington Consensus that Williamson uncovered was hardly one emanating from the majority of the people in this world, the supposed eventual beneficiaries of "development." Instead, neoliberalism provided an ideal environment for Wal-Mart, Ford, ExxonMobil, and the rest of the Fortune 500 to flourish as they spread their assembly lines, shopping malls, and American culture around the world. It was, by Williamson's definition, a consensus among elites, focused narrowly on catalyzing aggregate economic growth. As Williamson later acknowledged, "I deliberately excluded from [my] list [of the ten areas] anything which was primarily redistributive ... because I felt the Washington of the 1980s to be a city that was essentially contemptuous of equity concerns."[5] Likewise, explained Williamson, the Consensus "had relatively little to say about social issues ... and almost nothing to do with the environmental question."[6]

But in those countries where Consensus policies were actually applied, the on-the-ground impact almost never meshed with the theoretical propositions, even in terms of catalyzing economic growth. Moreover, those issues about which Williamson's "Washington of the 1980s" was "contemptuous" or had "little to say"—those issues of social, environmental, and political justice—turned out to matter a great deal to the supposed beneficiaries. And, indeed, as the era of market fundamentalism unfolded and its effects started to be felt on the ground, local "backlashes" emerged on every continent save Antarctica, initially to protest Consensus policies and subsequently to assert alternatives.

The first signs of resistance appeared in India, the Philippines, and several other countries in the 1970s, often where local communities rose up against World Bank incursions. After the World Bank proposed a series of dams across the Chico River in the northern Philippines, for example, the indigenous communities in the area took the unprecedented step of writing then World Bank president Robert McNamara to halt the flooding of their ancestral domain. They received no answer. The local people protested on the ground, meeting with violent reprisals from the authoritarian Marcos government. Still no answer from the World Bank. And so the local people resorted to a different technique: When the technical folks arrived, indigenous women bared their breasts in protest to keep the project from going forward.[7]

That was more than thirty years ago. Things have clearly changed since then in terms of formal and informal structures of protest and accountability. There are now sophisticated global and local civil-society campaigns focused on the World Bank and other public and private institutions that set the rules for global trade and investment. In Africa, Asia, Latin America, and the Caribbean, groups such as the Jubilee South debt cancellation network and the Hemispheric Social Alliance have become forceful actors on the global stage. Over time these backlashes and groups evolved into a global movement, a "movement of movements"—what those who are a part of it have called the global justice movement, the global backlash, globalization from below, the anti-corporate globalization movement, the alter-globalization movement, or the anti-globalization movement.[8] By the early 2000s, the World Social Forum gatherings were attracting more than 100,000 participants to an "alternative space" to explore, share, and build joint strategies around alternatives to the Washington Consensus.[9]

The clash of paradigms—Consensus versus alter-globalization movement—has now spanned nearly three decades. The Consensus, seemingly unstoppable in its advance from the mid-1980s to mid-1990s, now stands severely wounded. The alter-globalization movement can no longer be judged simply as a protest or defensive movement; its alternatives—alternatives in theory and in practice—can now be assessed on local, national, regional, and global levels.

Why This Book, and Why Now?

Let us repeat our earlier words: We stand at a moment marking the end of what may well be the most destructive development era of modern history. And so its story must be retold, because now we know not only the beginning but also the end—and we know the key historical markers in the middle. We can look back over the era, study the markers, and try to understand what happened and why.

While we are at the end of an era, one must be very careful to understand our word choice. We have not said that free-market policies are dead; rather, their reign as a consensus in Williamson's sense of the term has ended. Some key centers of power still subscribe to its religion, but the era of a prevailing paradigm is over.

Hence, it is a propitious moment to take stock. Understanding the rise and fall of the Washington Consensus is critical to understanding the suffering of billions of people in well over a hundred countries and the paths that are available to them in the future. This history is important in and of itself. But the historical evolution of neoliberalism, the evolving critiques of it, and the growth of a backlash of both citizen groups and some governments are critical to understanding the contemporary development debate—and the obstacles and possibilities of the current moment.

Why not simply start in the current period? Too often, the prevailing orthodoxy of development in theory and practice is presented ahistorically. Indeed, we would not be surprised if some of you reading these pages were unaware that there was ever a vibrant development debate or that "free-market fundamentalism" did not always reign.

We would argue that one cannot understand the end of the era by just standing in the current moment. Rather, one has to witness the dynamics up close, to touch ground at various moments during the past decades. To understand the current historical moment—and what we believe are its very positive possibilities and very real challenges—we must travel back in time.

Time travel allows us to discover the dynamics, the strengths, and the weaknesses of various sides of the development debate, as well as the convergences and divergences of different moments in history. Time travel allows us to witness moments of hope as well as moments of disappointment, moments at which things could have changed. You will see the holding power of the Consensus model—for example, how it maintained its dominance through power shifts in Washington. As you will see, in 1993 we held out hope that the new Clinton administration might move beyond the dominant paradigm. However, we discover that in 1995 and 1999 this dominant paradigm still transcended richer-country politics, and we analyze why.

Time travel is also vital so that we can learn the lessons—both positive and negative—from this era, and so that we can avoid the mistakes of the past as we chart the future. Understanding the rise and fall of this development orthodoxy and the rise of alternatives should also remind us that development rules and institutions—indeed, even paradigms—can be created and can be changed. They were in the 1940s. They were again in the early 1980s. They are being changed right now, and they can be changed again in the years to come.

U.S. president Harry Truman's secretary of state, Dean Acheson, immodestly described his moment in history marked by World War II and the immediate postwar years as his being "present at the creation" of the post–World War II global economy.[10] Today, we need to be aware that we are present at the creation of a new development era.

Thus, this book and its time travel.

Tour Guides

Because we two are the self-appointed tour guides for your time travel, we need to tell you more about ourselves. It was to our good fortunes to have come onto the development stage *before* the reign of the Washington Consensus. Indeed, unbeknownst to us, we each began the research for this book in the 1970s.

Our stories begin separately. For Robin, those pre–Consensus experiences included frequent sojourns to the Philippines, a country that was a prime early "guinea pig" of neoliberalism. Robin's development experiences started in the late 1970s when she spent that year in the southern Philippines, working with the indigenous community whose ancestral land was threatened. It was this experience that focused Robin's eyes on the human cost of so-called development and onto the global economic context of development. The forces behind investment, trade, and aid were outside the control of that indigenous community, yet these forces exercised a huge impact on the lives of individuals, their communities, and their environment.

John's story also begins in the 1970s. In 1977 he moved to Geneva, working at what was one of the most vibrant hubs of development activity and optimism in that pre–Consensus era: the UN Conference on Trade and Development (UNCTAD). There, at UNCTAD, global economic agreements were being negotiated among governments to try to ensure fair and stable prices for the key commodities on which poorer countries had come to depend—coffee, tea, sugar, tin, and others. John participated in meetings of representatives from cotton-producing and -consuming countries as they attempted to hammer out a price-stabilizing international cotton agreement. Despite the fact that the U.S. government delegation included executives of cotton-trading conglomerates hostile to the agreement, it was a time of hope and possibility in terms of changing the rules of the global economy. During this period, John developed expertise on transnational corporations at UNCTAD as well as at the World Health Organization, which, in the 1970s and early 1980s, turned a spotlight on the giant corporations that controlled the marketing of infant formula, tobacco, alcohol, and pharmaceuticals.

In the late 1970s, fresh from the Philippines and Switzerland, we met as graduate students at Princeton University, where we pursued "development studies." We were fortunate to begin our studies in the late 1970s—before the development dogma of the 1980s hardened into a firm ideology. We studied under (among others) Nobel Prize laureate W. Arthur Lewis, who encouraged us to follow the ever-changing global economy, as well as the possibilities and obstacles presented by technological change. We each found a mentor in international human-rights lawyer Richard Falk, who directed our intellectual gaze to the public and private institutions that steer the global economy.

Throughout our studies, we were encouraged to debate and to eschew facile answers to complicated problems. What really did "development" entail economically, socially, politically? How did colonial powers, global corporations, and public institutions such as the World Bank and the International Monetary Fund steer "development" (read: economic growth) toward the interests of the few? And what were the various paths to development? How was one to assess Kenya's free-market model, for example, versus Julius Nyerere's self-reliant path for Tanzania?

Being at centers of debate—in the rural Philippines, in the United Nations, and in our particular corner of academia—perhaps made us all the more sensitive to the changing winds of the official development debate.

As the era of neoliberalism began, Robin returned to the Philippines for another year to follow the negotiations between international donors and top Philippine government officials to reshape that country's policies to fit the Washington Consensus. Then, in the early 1980s, Robin witnessed the gelling of the Consensus from "insider" posts as an international economist working on the World Bank and the InterAmerican Development Bank at the U.S. Treasury Department (during the administration of Ronald Reagan). There, she was struck by the certainty of political appointees at Treasury about the unquestioned correctness of these policies. She went on to work on Third World debt as a staff economist in the U.S. Congress. She left the U.S. government in the mid-1980s—under a fellowship from the Council on Foreign Relations—to reflect and write on the narrowing development debate and on the international economic context for development.

As market fundamentalism gelled in the early 1980s, John moved to Washington, D.C., to work at the nonprofit Institute for Policy Studies (IPS). First as head of its global economy project and then as director of IPS, John has been in the middle of debates over debt, trade, and development. As part of his work, John advised groups that formed the global debt relief movement, and he helped bring together researchers and activists from North and South into the International Forum on Globalization to critique neoliberalism and pose alternatives. He was one of the roughly sixty thousand participants in the so-called Seattle Coalition that initiated the era of mass protests and teach-ins in November 1999 at a key global trade meeting. And, often with Robin, he joined other prior and subsequent demonstrations and meetings on globalization.

Travel Itinerary and Guide Book

It is a matter of some serendipity that our period of observing and writing together allowed us to observe the rise and fall of the Washington Consensus and witness (and participate in) the rise of the alter-globalization movement. We learned by traveling through it, by feeling, smelling, and tasting the protests and the alternatives of numerous parts of the backlash. The massive marches in places such as Seattle were a tribute to, and a result of, the enormous devastation of neoliberal policies on workers, who carried banners alongside farmers, environmentalists, women, students, and religious and health care activists. And, thus, as we stated, we are marking the end of the era by traveling through it again, this time with you.

Your trip itinerary in brief: The next six chapters chart the rise and fall of the Washington Consensus and the rise of its global critics. Each chapter is a resting point at a critical juncture as we travel through time and witness the Consensus's dramatic emergence (Chapter 2), the birth of the alter-globalization movement (Chapter 3), the addition of environment to the debate (Chapter 4), the Clinton administration's embrace of the Consensus (Chapter 5), the emergence of deep cracks in elite circles over the Consensus by the turn of the century (Chapter 6), and the attempt by elites to resuscitate the Consensus after September 11, 2001 (Chapter 7). We conclude with a chapter that addresses the prospects that a new "development era" can rise from the ashes of the old, and we offer a multifaceted "development" lens through which readers can view and assess new policies, rules, and institutions.

Each of the stops along the trip provides a we-were-there look on this constantly evolving development debate in theory and practice. As we travel, we focus on three key intersecting threads that each of the chapters addresses at a different moment in time over this twenty-year period:

1. What are the key tenets of this dominant development paradigm (interchangeably referred to as the Washington Consensus, market fundamentalism, or neoliberalism), who is behind it, and how is it being imposed on poorer countries? The chapters that follow start with the creation of World Bank "structural adjustment" loans in 1979–1980 and the onset of the debt crisis in 1982 as levers for imposing neoliberalism. The chapters proceed to watch and analyze as cracks emerge in the model in the late 1990s, and as events of September 11, 2001, bring a renewed burst of commitment to and rationalization for key aspects of the Washington Consensus approach among elite supporters.

2. What are the key myths of the "Washington Consensus" approach, and what have been its key flaws? Debates over neoliberalism erupted around the world in the 1990s and, although interrupted by September 11, continue right up to the present. These debates are heated and acrimonious, and many amount to nothing less than a clash of paradigms. In several of the chapters, we take on different sets of myths and faulty assumptions that were put forward by proponents of neoliberalism at various moments over the past two decades. In Chapter 2, we start with our critique of the approach in economic terms, disputing assumptions about how neoliberal policies would catalyze economic growth in the South. In Chapter 3, we challenge myths concerning the alleged social and economic benefits of neoliberalism. Chapter 4 zeroes in on myths about the ostensible benefits of neoliberalism for the environment. Chapter 5 counters myths about the purported closing of economic gaps within and among nations, and Chapter 7 challenges historical and newly resurrected myths about poverty as the problem and about "more aid" and "more trade" as solutions. The chapters also demonstrate where critics (including the authors) predicted severe flaws with this paradigm (for example, the surge of short-term financial flows that led to the Asian crisis in 1997) that, while dismissed by the proponents of the Washington Consensus, proved to be correct.

3. Who makes up the citizen backlash—or alter-globalization movement—and what is this movement proposing? The book offers you a front-row seat to watch the evolution of this global movement from its birth in the 1980s, to the growth of labor, environment, farm, religious, student, health, women, and other activists in the 1990s, to the emergence of governments in Latin America and elsewhere who opposed the dominant paradigm in the first decade of the 2000s. The chapters chart this evolution, and the evolution of a diverse menu of ever-more sophisticated alternative development proposals and institutions that emphasize dignified work, a clean environment, and healthy communities. A final chapter, written in 2008, sums up the best current thinking and initiatives of the alter-globalization movement at local, national, regional, and international levels.

Background for Your Travel: The Age of Debate (1960–1980)[11]

As mentioned above, we each entered the development debate during the previous era, the one that spanned the 1960s and 1970s. A few words on that era are necessary background for your time travel, which will start in the 1980s.

In the first three decades following World War II, particularly since 1960, there was a lively debate in many parts of the world over the respective roles of government and the market in the development process. During that period, most development scholars and practitioners did not believe there was a need for an overarching macroeconomic model—a cookie-cutter model—for all countries to follow. Indeed, the post–World War II decades of Keynesian economic thinking spread appreciation of different active roles that governments could play in steering economies, and various countries experimented in different ways. "We are all Keynesians," U.S. president Richard Nixon announced in 1971, with words that sound almost preposterous now.[12]

Prior to the 1980s, most developing countries favored a fairly strong governmental role in development planning and policies, fearing that unfettered markets in a world of unequal nations would put them at a disadvantage. In fact, most of these governments maintained trade restrictions of some sort and gave preferences to national over foreign investment. Regulating financial flows in and out of a country was the norm for both developing and developed countries.[13]

In many poorer nations, governments pursued different versions of what became known as "import-substitution industrialization," wherein they created incentives to help certain industries take off. This was partly rooted in research by Latin American economists—notably Argentine Raul Prebisch and his fellow "structuralists"—that poorer nations were structurally disadvantaged in the global economy by overreliance on exports of raw materials (both agricultural and mineral), given "declining terms of trade" whereby prices of such commodities tended to rise more slowly than those of the manufactured goods those poorer countries imported.[14]

By building up the capacity for industrial exports through, for example, processing cotton into textiles or petroleum into petrochemicals, these nations could eliminate that disadvantage. Some countries, such as Turkey, Mexico, and Brazil, had begun to pursue those policies during the Great Depression of the 1930s as world trade declined, and many more turned to these import-substitution policies in the 1960s and 1970s.

Meanwhile, in Africa in the 1960s and 1970s, a number of newly independent governments embraced what some called "African socialism," which borrowed from import substitution and mixed it with traditional African notions of society, collectivism, and the village economy.[15] The best known of these experiments was Tanzania under the flamboyant leader Julius Nyerere, who championed village-based self-reliance.[16]

These various models of national development, with strong governmental involvement, had their counterparts at the regional and global levels. At the regional level, countries in several parts of the world constructed regional trade blocs. The logic of these blocs was that several countries acting together could create "economies of scale" at a regional level. For example, the Nicaraguan economy was too small to support an automobile industry, but Central America could develop one if nations created a uniform external tariff and reduced trade barriers between the nations within the regional bloc. On this logic, cooperative trade agreements were created in the 1960s in Central America, the Caribbean, Andean nations, and East Africa.[17]

At a global level, in forums such as the UN Conference on Trade and Development with structuralist Raul Prebisch as its first secretary-general (and where John worked in the late 1970s and early 1980s), poor nations began to craft a global economic architecture as early as the 1960s. They gave an overarching name to these various proposals: the "new international economic order."[18] They argued that one could close the widening gap between rich and poor countries through collective government action to raise commodity prices and stimulate technology transfers and development assistance. A core pillar of this agenda was the range of international commodity agreements, such as the one on cotton on which John worked, to raise and stabilize prices.[19] Several of these agreements were put in place.

The popularity of such agreements among poor nations skyrocketed after 1974, when the world watched poorer oil-exporting nations form an organization, the Organization of Petroleum Exporting Countries (OPEC), which quickly managed to quadruple the global price of oil through supply management. Indeed, the rise and power of OPEC gave "power" to the New International Economic Order during the 1970s. But, as poor nations coalesced, key rich nations fought back. As the decade progressed, the U.S. government rallied rich country governments to oppose most of these proposals, and most were stalled by the early 1980s.

During the 1960s and 1970s, however, many economies grew rapidly by deploying a variety of these alternative approaches.[20] At the same time, the seeds of the later Washington Consensus were planted by economists such as the University of Chicago's Milton Friedman,[21] and politicians such as Arizona senator Barry Goldwater, the unsuccessful Republican U.S. presidential candidate in 1964. Friedman's "radical" free-market notions were given an incubator in the 1970s when Chilean general Augusto Pinochet seized power in a bloody coup in 1973. U.S. advisors, the notorious "Chicago-boys," were welcomed by the new dictator to apply free-market "shock therapy" to the formerly socialist Chile.[22] Free-market backers pointed to these policies' impact on dampening inflation and creating growth in certain parts of the economy. Other nations, such as Kenya, likewise began to experiment with free-market policies.

But still, there was a debate. And Kenya and Pinochet's Chile were rather lonely islands of free-market policies until the 1980s—until . . . well, let us leave that story for the next chapter, in which we travel back in time to the 1980s.

To meet the actors behind the Consensus and those who would crack it, put on your seatbelts. The next 100 or so pages are a ride through some of the most dramatic development history of recent times—a tale of individuals, of institutions, of power, and of coercion, and a tale of life and death issues for the poorer majority who inhabit this earth.

Chapter 2

The Washington Consensus Emerges

For our first trip back in time, we bring you to the late 1980s, and to a transformed development landscape. The world had shifted from where we left it in the 1970s, with Chile being among the few laboratories of Milton Friedman's free-market experiments to a world where market fundamentalism had become the reigning doctrine, not just in poorer nations but in richer ones as well.

How did this happen?

To set the scene: During the first half of the 1980s, backers of what the conservative U.S.–based Heritage Foundation would call the "free market silent revolution"[1] would take advantage of four phenomena to engineer a perfect storm for the rapid ascent of the Washington Consensus.

First, market fundamentalists spread a simplistic argument about the roots of a major problem: the unusually high levels of inflation experienced by many richer and poorer economies (including the United States) in the late 1970s. In some Latin American nations, this hyperinflation reached triple-digit levels. Many factors led to the inflation, including huge surges in oil prices during the 1970s. But free-market backers invariably pointed fingers at one culprit that conveniently served their purposes: "too much" government that spent "too much" money to implement import-substitution-industrialization (ISI) policies.

Add to this a second component, what should be called false advertising: As free-market pundits searched the world for success stories in the 1970s, they invariably discovered the rapidly growing, rapidly industrializing, and rapidly exporting nations of East Asia. Led by South Korea and Taiwan, these were termed the Asian Miracles, or Little Dragons, or Newly Industrializing Countries (NICs). Despite the fact that there was ample evidence to argue that the NICs included cases of import substitution working successfully, Washington Consensus proponents spread the erroneous story that the East Asian success was rooted in free-market policies.

Third came a fortuitous alignment of the stars politically with the election of the new leaders of the "free world": Margaret Thatcher in England (1979), Ronald Reagan in the United States (1981), and Helmut Kohl in Germany (1982). These new governments were united in championing free trade, free investment, deregulation, and privatization as the best antidote to inflation and the only route to growth. There was no alternative.

Fourth, the market fundamentalists found themselves with a powerful lever to impose Consensus policies on dozens of poorer nations: the debt crisis that erupted in 1982 (which we will watch evolve as we travel). That year, a large number of developing countries began to lose substantial control over their economies as foreign debts incurred during the preceding two decades fell due at a moment of historically high interest rates. As you will see, the United States and other rich country governments bestowed vast new powers on the World Bank and International Monetary Fund to spread neoliberalism by requiring indebted nations to earn these institutions' "seal of approval" as a condition for new loans.

And so, with this quadruple convergence of the early 1980s to set the scene, we begin our travels to examine the development debate toward the end of the decade when the Washington Consensus became the dogma of the development establishment. Robin's research in the Philippines earlier in the decade adds country-specific examples to our assessment, and a sense of urgency to our critique.

A note on semantics here: We touch ground in 1988 just before the term "Washington Consensus" was to be coined; the rhetoric of 1988 focused on the need for developing countries to implement a package of market-oriented "structural" adjustments that were said to mimic those used by the so-called newly industrializing countries, or NICs.

As we travel back to the late 1980s, you will also discover that, by and large, the global citizen backlash to the market fundamentalist policies of the Bank and Fund was still in its infancy. Indeed, the alter-globalization movement hardly appears in the rest of this chapter. At this time, the alternatives focused on by critics, including ourselves, were still very much government-centric—

reflecting the strong influence of Keynes and Prebisch on those who did not accept the Consensus in its first decade.

Let the curtain open to 1988, to witness the rise of neoliberalism and the growing power of the public institutions that propelled it forward.

☆——☆

1988—Throughout the 1980s, the most common policy advice to developing countries the world over was to follow a simple formula: Copy the export-oriented path of the newly industrializing countries, the celebrated NICs. These economies—Brazil, Hong Kong, Mexico, Singapore, South Korea, and Taiwan—burst onto world manufactures' markets in the late 1960s and the 1970s. By 1978, these six economies plus India accounted for fully 70 percent of the developing world's manufactured exports. Their growth rates for gross national product (GNP) and exports were unequaled.

No wonder the call was sounded for others to follow. Dozens have tried. But with the possible exceptions of Malaysia and Thailand, no country has come close. Why not? The answer lies in far-reaching changes in the global economy—from synthetic substitutes for commodity exports to unsustainable levels of external debt—that have created a glut economy offering little room for new entrants.

Despite these shifts, the foremost international development institutions, the World Bank and the International Monetary Fund (IMF), continue to promote the NIC path as the way for heavily indebted developing countries to escape the debt crisis. Yet in 1988, eight years into a period of reduced growth in world markets, the bankruptcy of this approach should be all too apparent. By the end of the 1970s, the World Bank had singled out the four Asian NICs as models to be studied by a second rung of developing countries. Having mastered the production of textiles, clothing, shoes, simple consumer electronics, and other light-manufactured wares, these four NICs were moving into more sophisticated products like automobiles and videocassette recorders. Therefore, the Bank argued, as the NICs' level of industrial development advanced, they would abandon the more basic industries to other countries. As Bela Balassa, a prominent, longtime Bank consultant, asserted, the NICs would "upgrade and … diversify their exports in line with their changing comparative advantage," leaving "countries at lower stages of industrial development [to] replace exports of unskilled-labor-intensive commodities from the newly industrializing countries to industrial country markets."[2]

But the World Bank did more than offer the intellectual underpinnings for this development theory. In the late 1970s it positioned itself as a central actor in pushing the would-be NICs up the ladder to the NIC rung. In

May 1979, then World Bank president Robert McNamara, in an address to a United Nations Conference on Trade and Development (UNCTAD) meeting in Manila, called for developing countries to "upgrade their export structure to take advantage of the export markets being vacated by more advanced developing countries." McNamara added that the Bank would move to the forefront of this new "program of action." To do so, however, the Bank needed to move beyond its more traditional microlevel project lending with a new instrument that would maximize its leverage with developing countries. Loans for hydroelectric dams, highways, and urban renewal, among other projects, had made the Bank the key international development player, but they did not confer on the Bank adequate leverage for the proposed global restructuring.

Consequently, the Bank turned to a new set of policy prescriptions, dubbed "structural adjustment," the key ingredient of which was structural adjustment loans (SALs). These large balance-of-payments loans—targeted toward broad sectors and heavily conditioned on a recipient's economic reforms—sought to hasten the new international division of labor whereby the would-be NICs would mimic the established NICs' light-manufactures export successes. The SALs were "the World Bank's best weapon yet," as a close aide of McNamara said in 1981.[3] These 1980s SALs carried a broad set of policy prescriptions that focused on trade-related economic sectors; they were designed to enhance efficiency and export orientation.[4]

Who are these would-be NICs that the World Bank and the IMF hoped to push up the development ladder? According to various classification systems, including those of the World Bank, this group comprises up to thirty second-tier less developed countries (LDCs) across Africa, Asia, and Latin America.[5]

These would-be NICs largely received the big loans and amplified attention from the Bank during the late 1970s and early 1980s. Of the nine countries rewarded with a structural adjustment loan of more than $50 million as of mid-1982, seven were would-be NICs and one was a NIC. Moreover, the IMF's attention largely complemented the Bank's. Of the twenty countries that by mid-1982 had received one of the IMF's extended fund facilities—highly conditioned loans with a ten-year repayment period—of more than $50 million, twelve fell into the would-be NICs grouping and two were NICs.

More insight into the Bank's role in the would-be NICs can be gained by looking at one illuminating case, the Philippines—a country that was, as former Central Bank governor Gregorio Licaros phrased it to one of the authors in 1980, the "guinea pig" for structural adjustment.[6] By the fall of the Ferdinand Marcos dictatorship in February 1986, the Philippines had borrowed more than \$4.5 billion from the World Bank in more than 100 project and program loans. And, in 1980, the Bank finalized a first Philippine SAL package.

With this \$200 million loan, the government committed itself to a group of "structural adjustment" policies stipulating an export-oriented course for Philippine industry. Former high-ranking Philippine officials, including both proponents and opponents of the reforms, agree that the SAL's policies marked a critical juncture in the Philippine development path. Tariffs were slashed. Protective import restrictions were lifted. The exchange rate began a steady and steep devaluation, while export- and investment-promotion policies diverted resources from domestically oriented output. New free-trade tax havens, using generous incentives for transnational corporations (TNCs) to exploit low-cost Filipino labor, were established across the archipelago. Individual light-manufacturing industries, such as textiles, cement, food processing, furniture, and footwear, were slated for restructuring according to World Bank specifications.

During this period, similar policies were pushed by the World Bank in other would-be NICs. World Bank SALs to the Ivory Coast, Kenya, Pakistan, Senegal, and Turkey—like the Philippine SAL—all concentrated on improving export incentives and performance.

NIC Rivalry

In effect the World Bank was helping to create a group of countries that would compete against each other to become NICs. The result was two vicious battles—one to offer cheaper, more docile labor forces and more attractive financial incentives to lure global corporations' assembly lines away from the other countries, and the other to win scarce export markets.

Sri Lanka's advertisement in the October 16, 1981, issue of the *Far Eastern Economic Review* said it well: "Sri Lanka challenges you to match the advantages of its Free Trade Zone, against those being offered elsewhere.... Sri Lanka has the lowest labor rates in Asia." Variations on that appeal were issued by one would-be NIC after another, putting global corporations in a choice position from which to bargain the most lucrative investment or subcontracting deals.

The competition encouraged labor repression and exploitation. One Manila-based global-corporate executive explained in a 1981 interview: "We tell the [Philippine] government: you've got to clamp down [on labor].... Or we threaten to move elsewhere. And we'll do just that. There's Sri Lanka [and] now China too."

Most of the Bank's public documents sought to play down the problems associated with rivalry among the would-be NICs. But the Bank was not unaware of the potential zero-sum game. In a January 1979 working paper assessing the LDCs' manufacturing export potential, two leading Bank economists, Hollis Chenery and Donald Keesing, forecast that "the increasing number of successful competitors may make it increasingly difficult for newcomers to get established" and that the success of a "few" could leave "too little" opportunity for the rest.

Yet who had set in motion this chain of competition? An October 1979 World Bank report had counseled the Philippines to take advantage of the fact that its wages had "declined significantly relative to those in competing ... countries," notably Hong Kong and South Korea.[7] Almost simultaneously, as reported in the *Southeast Asia Chronicle* in December 1981, the Bank helped steer Indonesia onto a parallel course, advising that "incentives for firms to locate there rather than in some other Southeast Asian country ... must be provided." Meanwhile, Sri Lanka received a $20 million World Bank loan to establish a new export platform for apparel subcontracting and the Bank pushed the People's Republic of China (PRC), Thailand, and some of the Caribbean Basin countries into the light-manufactures arena as well.

The competition among would-be NICs was further exacerbated by the exporters of an earlier era, the Asian NICs of Hong Kong, Singapore, South Korea, and Taiwan. World Bank theory to the contrary, these countries were not abandoning textiles, apparel, and electronics assembly as they moved into higher stages of industrialization. Indeed, since the 1960s, the Asian NICs had been spreading throughout the entire range of industry—from light to heavy, from unsophisticated to sophisticated—leaving little space for would-be NICs.

The export performance of the Asian NICs between 1979 and 1985 illustrates this point. Their combined exports leaped from $60.5 billion to $113.9 billion, a stunning 88 percent increase during years of slow global economic growth. More sophisticated "strategic" industries like telecommunications, complex electronic equipment, and motor vehicles were encouraged by NIC governments through various tax holidays and subsidized loans.

On a regular basis, export surges in these high value-added industries captured newspaper headlines. Little attention was paid, however, to the continuing rapid NIC export growth in traditional light manufactures. Through a combination of innovation, cost-cutting measures, upgrading capital equipment, and state and private-sector cooperation, these countries held on to and expanded their markets. Textile and clothing exports from the four grew from \$14.6 billion to \$23.4 billion over the six years, a 60 percent rise.

Another factor also was inhibiting the would-be NICs' economic ascension—new technologies. The more than a decade that separated the NICs' debut from that of the would-be NICs witnessed technological advances in several sectors that changed the very definition of Third World industrialization.

By the late 1970s, technological innovations, led by the microprocessor revolution, made the global fragmentation of production highly profitable and desirable. Whereas the original NICs had received complete industrial processes such as shipbuilding and machinery, the would-be NICs won marginal segments of scattered assembly lines for semiconductors and consumer electronics, textiles and apparel. In Sri Lanka, for example, workers in export-processing zones used basic sewing machines to stitch together garments from imported fabric. In the Philippines, female workers in 1980 were performing only one of the ten major operations of electronic production, attaching hairlike gold wires to silicon chips.

As a result, these new global assembly lines left gaping disparities between the gross value of the would-be NICs' industrial export earnings and the actual value added to the product in the developing country. Consider again the Philippine case. With the Philippines importing cartons for its banana exports, cans for some food exports, and a wide assortment of machinery and component parts for its limited apparel and electronic assembly line—domestic "value added" in most Philippine industries was quite low. As a confidential 1981 World Bank report revealed, for every dollar of nontraditional-export earnings, only 25 cents stayed in the Philippines; the rest was siphoned off by import payments.[8]

If the production side of the would-be NIC experience offered less than what was advertised, the marketing side was even grimmer. For light-manufactured exports to be the engine for the would-be NICs, world trade—that is, global demand for these products—had to grow each year. There was no way to escape this logic in the aggregate.

But in the late 1970s and early 1980s, at precisely the time when would-be NICs were induced to embark on a nontraditional-export path, these necessary conditions were decidedly absent. Over the decade from 1963 to 1973, the volume of world exports rose at a rapid average annual rate of 8.5 percent. Beginning in 1973, however, an economic deceleration slowed the average annual expansion to 4 percent. By 1980 exports were crawling ahead at only 1 percent per year, and in 1981 they slowed to no growth.

Behind these global trade statistics lurked the domestic stagnation of the industrialized economies. According to IMF figures, from 1976 to 1979 the real GNP of industrialized countries grew at a tolerable average yearly rate of 4 percent. By 1980, Oganization for Economic Cooperation and Development (OECD) growth was limping ahead at only 1.25 percent; the next year it increased again by only 1.25 percent. These two years presaged a decade of vastly reduced growth. From 1981 to 1985 world output slowed to an average of 2.7 percent per year and trade to 2.8 percent.[9]

As more countries battled for the same tepid export markets, prices plunged. Between 1981 and 1985, world prices of food commodities fell at an average annual rate of 15 percent; agricultural raw materials dropped at an average annual rate of 7 percent; and minerals and metals fell 6 percent. The year 1986 proved even dimmer, when a 30 percent decline in the developing countries' terms of trade (the ratio of prices of developing-country exports to prices of their imports) translated into a staggering $594 billion to the developed world.

Another pitfall facing the LDCs' export-oriented industrialization was the panoply of quantitative restrictions that had spread to cover fully one-half of global trade. Despite official encomiums to "free trade," the richer countries increasingly were barricading themselves behind what even President Reagan's Council of Economic Advisers admitted in their 1982 annual report were "neomercantile" policies.

These defensive machinations to moderate the recessionary bite at home were baptized the "new protectionism"—a proliferation of American, European, and Japanese trade barriers, notably quotas on poorer countries' manufactured exports. "New" referred to the dazzling array of nontariff barriers not regulated by the General Agreement on Tariffs and Trade. Voluntary export restraints and orderly marketing arrangements flourished. As the World Bank and the IMF encouraged free-trade policies on poorer nations, the major voting blocs within those institutions retreated from any semblance of free trade at home.

By the calculations of the World Bank's own economists in 1979, the most dangerous of the new protectionist barriers was centered in the apparel, textile, and footwear sectors.[10] Yet it was precisely these sectors—along with furniture, wood products, electronics, and other light-manufactured exports—that the Bank had pinpointed as the engine of growth for the would-be NICs. The restrictive allotments of the Multi-Fiber Arrangement made textiles and apparel perhaps the most heavily controlled sectors in international trade. As a result, the poorer countries' share of textile and apparel exports began to shrink in the early 1980s.

Yet in the late 1970s and early 1980s Bank officials who were planning Third World development strategies continually made assumptions that ignored slow growth and rising protectionism. Their model, grounded in theories of free trade and comparative advantage, posited the absence of such conditions. They opted instead for what was termed "one set of reasonable assumptions" without explaining their legitimacy. The set of "reasonable" assumptions about trade and protectionism that underpinned the Bank's structural adjustment reports and advice to would-be NICs was some permutation of the following: Industrial countries were to grow 4 percent annually in the 1980s, "worldwide economic recovery" stood on the horizon, and "no major set-backs" would occur in major markets.[11]

Did Bank economists really believe this? In the Philippine example a wide chasm between these assumptions and the private assessments of Bank officials was revealed time and again during interviews conducted by one of the authors in the early 1980s. One World Bank consultant and member of the Bank's appraisal mission for its first Philippine SAL, John Power, privately admitted his doubts about a successful outcome of Philippine export-oriented industrialization given the gravity of the "world situation." Yet a 1979 book he coauthored as background for the Philippine SAL, *Industrial Promotion Policies in the Philippines,* refused to give credence to any such misgivings.

The potential effects of this unsubstantiated optimism about the Philippines and other would-be NICs were never seriously considered by Bank officials. The development prescriptions of Bank officials were transformed into a kind of dogma: "The more hostile the external environment, the more urgent" the need for restructuring, an August 1980 *Report and Recommendation* urged. [12] In one instance, a Bank director took the floor at the executive board's final meeting on the Philippine SAL to question the management's scenario of Philippine "dynamic" export-led growth in light of "an adverse environment [including] lower than projected growth rates in industrial countries and increased protectionism." The board chairman's response epitomized the Bank's unquestioning attitude: "If the environment turned out to be more adverse than projected, then the ultimate benefits under the adjustment program would be reduced, but the nature of the adjustment needed would not be changed."[13] But such a response was no more than conjecture. No hard evidence and computer runs were offered to answer what should have been a basic question: If world trade did not grow, and if key markets became increasingly protected, would export-oriented industrialization be the optimal route to growth?

Between 1978 and 1987, the Bank consistently has projected average developing-country export growth rates of more than 5 percent per year; between 1981 and 1986 the actual annual growth rates (according to the United Nations) averaged instead a negative 0.4 percent. Why was a more accurate scenario not used? The 1978 *World Development Report* explained,

"Still lower growth rates are not considered here, not only because they are thought unlikely, but also because they would be associated with structural changes in trade and other relations between countries that could not be captured in the present analytical framework."

In other words, the World Bank had no vision of development in a world economy of curtailed growth. To a large extent Bank officials had equated growth with development. To them, development did not primarily mean providing adequate food, clean water, clothing, and housing—in short, offering a standard of living consistent with human dignity. Those had become secondary concerns to be met through growth. In the Bank's view, no economic growth meant no development and therefore could not be considered seriously.

In 1986, several years after the rosy predictions, the Bank conducted a confidential review of structural adjustment lending in which it acknowledged that "the impact of the adjustment programs on a country's economic performance has generally remained below expectations." This was an understatement. Through the 1970s all but one of the thirty would-be NICs had registered average growth in the value of exports of more than 12 percent annually. From 1980 to 1985—the first five years of SALs—only seven experienced export growth rates above 4 percent; nine, including the Philippines, suffered negative growth. The Bank report stumbled over what it called an "important reason" for the poor performance: "The world economic environment deteriorated to a much larger extent than foreseen." The document's suggestions for correcting this "overoptimism" may shock some in developing countries who thought they were heeding the advice of development experts: "The Bank should go beyond giving textbook solutions. The practical problems of implementation and the applicability of recommendations to specific country circumstances should be investigated.... This work needs to be supplemented with a more rigorous analysis at the country level of . . . the likely impact of the world economic environment on the domestic economy." [14]

A New World Economy

World Bank forecasts notwithstanding, global stagnation is likely to prove harder to shake than most would like to believe. Aside from protectionist pressures, a series of corporate developments has stunted demand globally, leaving increasing numbers of people at the margins of market activity—even should aggregate economic growth return to higher levels. Prominent among these developments are the commercial banks' handling of the Third

World debt crisis, corporate substitution for Third World raw materials, and labor-saving technological innovations in the developed world.

The debt crisis arose from heavy borrowing for infrastructure that in many countries fed corruption and capital flight. In the early 1980s, as oil prices and interest rates rose and primary commodity prices fell, country after country announced its inability to service debts owed to banks in the developed world. In rapid succession, the creditor banks sent these countries through IMF austerity programs, which prescribed a kind of shock treatment to bring countries' balance of payments out of deficit. Wage freezes, currency devaluations, and government spending cuts reduced imports into the Third World; indeed, many countries "successfully" wiped out trade and national budget deficits within a few years. But lowered wages and imports also dampened global economic growth.

Technological breakthroughs in substitutes for Third World raw materials also hurt growth performance in the developing world. A single anecdote typifies the impact of longer-term corporate development on commodity markets. Until 1981 the largest consumer of the world's sugar was Coca-Cola. That year, in a move rapidly emulated by other soft drink giants, Coca-Cola began to shift its sweetener from sugar to corn syrup. Western consumers might not have viewed the change as significant to them, but it displaced millions of Third World sugar workers for a product produced within industrial countries.

Advances in plastics, synthetic fibers, food chemistry, and biotechnology are bringing similar far-reaching changes to other raw materials and commodity markets. Cumulatively these substitutions have pushed tens of millions of Third World workers into the margins of the marketplace, further curbing global demand.

Likewise, new corporate technologies are transforming developed-country economies. The computer revolution, the major technological breakthrough of the 1960s–1980s, is strikingly dissimilar from earlier technological breakthroughs. The advent of electricity and the automobile, for example, generated millions of jobs in related industries and sparked economic booms in the leading countries. The microprocessor revolution has also created millions of jobs. However, applications of microprocessors have spread through almost every manufacturing and service sector in uses that are labor saving. Bank tellers, supermarket check-out clerks, assembly-line workers, and others are all joining the ranks of the unemployed. This phenomenon is reflected in Western Europe, where for seventeen straight years the unemployment rate has risen.

The result of these three changes is that, all over the world, industry is turning out more than consumers can buy. The new global glut economy coexists with billions of people with enormous needs and wants but with little ability to buy.

As world economic growth has slowed, so did the Third World activities of its central private institutions: global corporations and banks. Much of the growth of the 1960s and 1970s was based on a rapid expansion of production around the world by subsidiaries of such firms as Ford, John Deere, and Texas Instruments. Western banks followed to provide financing. Then, after 1973, they became major economic actors in the developing world in their own right as recyclers of billions of petrodollars.

As of the late 1980s, this is no longer the case. Banks and corporations go where there is growth and hence profit. Over the 1980s, the Third World basically stopped growing; many countries even slipped backward. Consequently, U.S. banks returned home for new short-term rewards—consumer credit, corporate mergers, and the get-rich-quick gimmicks of financial speculation.

Again, the statistics are stark. In 1983, international bank lending to developing countries, excluding offshore bank centers, totaled $35 billion. By 1985 a mere $3 billion in new lending had trickled in.

Unfortunately, the drop-off in bank and corporate involvement and the factors that spelled a longer-term slowdown did not seem to influence the policy advice of the World Bank and the IMF. The push to create a second tier of NICs began in the late 1970s and continued through 1982. It was derailed somewhat for the three-year period beginning in August 1982, when Mexico's declaration that it was unable to service its debts signaled the start of the debt crisis. That three-year spell was dominated by IMF austerity measures; close to 100 Fund loan agreements went into force.

By 1985, however, austerity had bred considerable resistance across the Third World. The United States responded in October 1985 with a plan proposed by Treasury Secretary James Baker. Although it seized the political initiative from the Latin American debtors, the Baker plan offered little that was new. Troubled debtors still were advised to go to the IMF for restructuring advice. To buttress the Fund, however, the World Bank was brought center stage and asked to pledge billions of dollars in new loans to the fifteen most troubled debtors, eleven of which were would-be NICs.[15]

The World Bank lost no time in advancing its version of development. If the debt crisis could be used as a lever, all the better. The Baker plan offered debtor countries similar amounts of new private lending if they complied with a combination of IMF austerity and World Bank structural adjustments of privatizing industry, liberalizing trade, and encouraging foreign investment, among other requirements. By the end of 1985, the Bank had granted broad SALs to twelve of the fifteen Baker plan countries.

Avoiding the Sin of Universality

Yet the changing world economy has created a desperate need to rethink the kinds of adjustments that will produce growth and development. At the very least, the adjustment strategies must be built on realistic assumptions. The East Asian NICs were the product of a radically different world economy. That they cannot be replicated in the 1980s is an indication of how much that world economy has changed.

Rather than increasing their reliance on the hostile world environment of the 1980s, developing countries should try to reduce this dependence and to diversify trading partners and products. This approach implies a careful restructuring of trade and financial linkages to conform with a development logic that is driven by internal economic forces.

If economies can no longer be pulled along primarily by external growth, stronger internal buying power must be generated. The great challenge is to transform crushing social needs into effective demand and then to meet that demand by turning first to domestically produced goods and services, next to the region, and only after that to the wider world market. In most developing countries this development framework implies vast internal adjustment quite different from the World Bank's brand of structural adjustment. Most of the Third World's people cannot afford to purchase many goods and services. Wages are locked into rock-bottom subsistence rates; wealth and income are heavily skewed toward a relatively small, wealthy elite. As a result, spreading income more evenly requires, for a start, extensive land reform, progressive taxation policies, and guarantees of worker rights.

To offer more specifics on internal demand-driven development strategies is risky. Vastly different resource bases and social strata among countries suggest that a country-specific approach is essential. Indeed, the sin of universality in development strategies was perhaps the central weakness of IMF and World Bank adjustment programs.

Agrarian reform remains the major means of redistributing wealth and income and thereby increasing the effective purchasing power of the rural population. This is, interestingly enough, a lesson that the World Bank and the IMF chose not to learn from the South Korean and Taiwanese experiences. The people in Third World rural areas are largely either poor tenants or agricultural workers who earn only subsistence wages. They have meager resources to consume in the marketplace. Only through agrarian reform can this population begin to produce a surplus that can be translated into consumption. In economic terms, small farmers have a higher "marginal propensity" to consume than larger ones, and much of their consumption could be satisfied by locally produced products.

In a highly interdependent world, such demand-centered development does not and cannot imply autarky. What cannot be produced locally is produced nationally. What cannot be produced nationally is purchased from regional partners—which suggests the importance of revitalizing regional integration institutions. Only for those products where regional producers cannot satisfy demand is trade necessary with countries on the other side of the globe. Domestic needs should shape trade patterns rather than vice versa.

A 1987 United Nations report should provoke some rethinking in the would-be NICs. The *World Economic Survey 1987* offers the results of a statistical survey of the fastest growing developing countries over the slow-growth first half of the 1980s. Fourteen countries achieved per capita gross domestic product growth rates of more than 2.5 percent over this period; eight of them pursued policies oriented inwardly more than outwardly.

Leading the pack was China. Although this period saw the Chinese begin opening up to the world market, the country's economic growth was overwhelmingly domestic. Chinese rural industries, for example, grew at more than 20 percent annually during the 1980s. The extraordinarily rapid Chinese economic growth was attributable in good part to policy shifts since 1978 from central planning toward market incentives for production. Still, China's success was cushioned by a vast internal market made up of between 20 percent and 25 percent of the world's population whose real incomes had risen slowly in the decades after the PRC was established in 1949. Thus China's experience appears to make a case for opening up an economy slowly and only after a substantial domestic market has been developed and nurtured.

Most observers continue to view the Asian NICs as role models. And they offer glowing imagery in support of their view: Asian NICs have "already taken off," and the rest of the noncommunist Southeast Asian countries are "on the runway revving" up to follow, as former Japanese foreign minister Saburo Okita has described it.[16]

The would-be NICs have fallen for such prophecies for nearly a decade. Now, at the end of the 1980s, the time has come to demand not imagery but a realistic assessment of options. The debate on adjustment and development should be reopened; strategies that proclaim that the only option is greater dependence on an increasingly hostile and turbulent world economy need to be challenged. It is time to ask whether any more developing countries can really hope to become the South Korea or the Hong Kong of the 1990s.

Chapter 3

The Citizen Backlash Erupts
(with Walden Bello)

You have just finished a trip with us to the late 1980s. There, in a chapter that subjected the Washington Consensus to critique, we concluded that there were serious external constraints to a model that encouraged nations to shift resources toward exports—from growing protectionism in richer countries to increased substitution for raw-material exports. But our critique was hardly the dominant view. Instead, the Washington Consensus continued to expand, gaining great momentum and converts in the process.

Its increasing influence on the ground gave us—alas—more empirical fodder with which to expand our critique. By 1990, when we touch down again in the chapter that follows, we focus on an additional set of criticisms: Washington Consensus policies in practice damaged environments, worsened structural inequities, bypassed popular participation, and failed even in their very narrow goal of helping economies grow. And, alongside the Consensus's successful proselytizing, came a countermovement: As democratic movements expanded across the world, many people were rejecting the profoundly undemocratic nature of this approach.

Our 1990 critique displays palpable anger—undoubtedly reflecting the fact that we spent 1988 to 1989 living with citizen activists across the Philippines who were the victims of Consensus policies. You will meet some of these people in the pages that follow. This experience did not just make the devastation more real to us; it also broadened our sights to hundreds of other groups around the world that were the initial front of an alter-globalization movement, as you will see in this chapter. To amplify the on-the-ground insights and not lose sight of the NICs and the story of their purported "success," we invited Filipino scholar and activist Walden Bello to be a coauthor for this piece. Walden added his insights from fieldwork in South Korea and Taiwan, where he found himself on the frontlines of a citizen backlash centered on labor and environmental activism.

These movements did not become real to most of the public until nine years after this piece was written, when television cameras spread images of the so-called Seattle coalition of workers, environmentalists, farmers, and others who shut down a World Trade Organization meeting in Seattle, Washington. But, to us in 1990, they were already highly visible on the ground in the Philippines, South Korea, Taiwan, and elsewhere. And we found ourselves musing their future trajectory from our 1990s perspective: Might these movements, we ask in the chapter that follows, elect new governments that would challenge neoliberal policies in the years to come in such countries as South Africa, Brazil, and the Philippines? As you will see when we continue our travels into the 1990s, they indeed would in the first two.

Between our first time travel in 1988 and this one, another key moment occurs: the fall of the Berlin Wall in 1989 and, with it, the demise of one set of state-centered development models. Backers of the Washington Consensus tried to use the fall of the Berlin Wall as vindication of the free-market approach of the Consensus. Here we find one of our instances of missed opportunity; instead of misplaced triumphalism, the fall of the Berlin Wall could have opened up the development debate.

Finally, in this piece, we attempt to lay out the positive roles that government can play in the development process as a counter to the "government-bashing" that was so prevalent during this time. Then, as now, we believe there is a correct mix of government, markets, and civil society, different in each country, that is the key to successful development. In 1990, these words were treated like heresy by most of the development establishment.

⚜ — ⚜

1990—As the 1990s begin, the development debate has all but disappeared in the West. Monumental changes in Eastern Europe are widely interpreted as proof of the superiority of development models that are led by the private sector and oriented toward exports. Free–market capitalism is said to have prevailed because it alone promises growth and democracy for the battered economies of Africa, Asia, and Latin America. World Bank president Barber Conable summed up this prevailing view in remarks made in February 1990: "If I were to characterize the past decade, the most remarkable thing was the generation of a global consensus that market forces and economic efficiency were the best way to achieve the kind of growth which is the best antidote to poverty."[1]

Ample evidence exists, however, to suggest caution in the face of triumphalism. Warning signs are surfacing in South Korea and Taiwan, the miracle models of capitalist development. After decades of systematic exploitation, the South Korean labor force erupted in thousands of strikes during the late 1980s, undermining the very basis of that country's export success. Meanwhile, decades of uncontrolled industrial development have left large parts of Taiwan's landscape with poisoned soil and toxic water.

Additional evidence reveals extensive suffering throughout Africa, parts of Asia, and Latin America, where privatized adjustment has been practiced for more than a decade in a world economy of slower growth. As the United Nations Children's Fund noted in its 1990 annual report, "Over the course of the 1980s, average incomes have fallen by 10 per cent in most of Latin America and by over 20 percent in sub-Saharan Africa. . . . In many urban areas, real minimum wages have declined by as much as 50 per cent." The World Bank estimates that as many as 950 million of the world's 5.2 billion people are "chronically malnourished"—more than twice as many hungry people as a decade ago.[2]

In Latin America, people are talking about a lost decade, even a lost generation. In Rio de Janeiro, the lack of meaningful futures has given birth to a new sport: train surfing. Brazilian street children stand atop trains beside a 3,300 volt cable that sends trains hurtling at speeds of 120 kilometers per hour. During an eighteen-month period in 1987–1988, train surfing in Rio produced some 200 deaths and 500 gruesome injuries. "It's a form of suicide," said the father of a *surfista* who was killed. "Brazilian youth is suffering so much, they see no reason to live."[3]

This generalized failure of development in the 1980s is producing a very different kind of consensus among people the development establishment rarely contacts and whose voices are seldom heard. A new wave of democratic movements across Africa, Asia, and Latin America is demanding another kind of development. Through citizens' organizations, millions of environmentalists, farmers, women, and workers are saying they want to define and control their own futures. They are beginning to lay the groundwork for a new type of development—one that emphasizes ecological sustainability, equity, and participation, in addition to raising material living standards.

The false impression that the free-market model has triumphed in development is rooted in three misconceptions about the past decade:

- that the newly industrializing countries (NICs) of East Asia were exceptions to the "lost decade" and continue to represent models of successful development;
- that socialist command economies in Eastern Europe or the developing world failed principally because they did not use market mechanisms;
- that the export-oriented structural adjustment reforms that were put in place in much of the developing world have laid the groundwork for sustained growth in the 1990s.

The NICs did achieve the fastest growth rates among developing countries over the last three decades. But as the Berlin Wall was dismantled, the costs of high-speed, export-oriented industrialization were beginning to catch up with South Korea and Taiwan. The foundations of these supposed miracles of capitalist development were cracking.

In South Korea centralized authoritarian development has created a virtual time bomb. From afar, South Korea's spectacular growth may seem to have justified so-called transitional costs like severe labor repression. But many South Korean workers feel differently. Taking advantage of a small democratic opening between 1987 and 1989, more than 7,200 labor disputes broke out, compared with only 1,026 from 1981 through 1986. No major industry was spared; over the 1987–1988 period the number of unions increased two and a half times. In perhaps the best known confrontation, 14,000 policemen stormed the Hyundai shipyard in March 1989 to put down a 109-day strike.

The priority of many South Korean workers is not the maintenance of Korea's export competitiveness but rather acquiring what they regard as their overdue share of the fruits from three decades of growth.[4]

While a resentful labor movement threatens South Korea's traditional growth model by demanding greater equity and participation, a powerful environmental movement in Taiwan is challenging the island's fragile social consensus on export-oriented growth. This decentralized multiclass movement comprises consumers, farmers, influential intellectuals, residents of polluted areas, and workers. Although less publicized than Eastern Europe's environmental devastation, Taiwan's is also severe and results from the same technocratic assumption that "some" environmental damage is the necessary price of economic growth. As it turned out, "some" damage included at least 20 percent of the country's farmland, now polluted by industrial waste. Dumping of industrial and human waste (only 1 percent of the latter receives even primary treatment) has been unregulated. Uncontrolled air pollution has also contributed to a quadrupling of asthma cases among Taiwanese children in the last decade. Such numbers go a long way to explain why large segments of the populations of Korea and Taiwan now reject the path to growth long touted as a model for the Third World. Indeed, according to one 1985 survey, 59 percent of Taiwanese favor environmental protection over economic growth.[5]

These points do not mean that South Korea and Taiwan are about to become basket cases. Nor does the argument deny that they experienced periods of economic growth greater than that of most other developing countries. Instead, the evidence demonstrates that both countries can no longer practice a growth strategy based on repression of workers and abuse of the environment. It is now clear that each would have been better off trading some economic growth for more democracy and more ecological sensitivity from the start. Korea and Taiwan hardly serve as exemplary models for development.

While the cracks in the NIC model of development have been largely ignored in the West, the failure of socialism as an agent of development has been overplayed. There is no disputing this model's collapse; one cannot argue with the millions who have taken to the streets across Eastern Europe. Yet an overlay of the NICs' experience with that of Eastern Europe suggests a less facile explanation for the failure of socialism than blaming it solely on the suppression of market mechanisms.

During the 1960s in Eastern Europe, the government-led "command" economies achieved growth rates higher than those of the capitalist world, according to a 1984 United Nations Conference on Trade and Development report, while building the infrastructure for further industrial advance.[6] Only the Japanese, who seem less blinded by free-market ideology and more appreciative of the role of a centralized state, have reconciled the two models for a more insightful lesson. As an editorial in the *Japan Times* argued in December 1989:[7]

> Communism has never been a complete failure, nor has capitalism been a complete success. If there are any lessons to be gleaned from the events of 1989, they do not point to a total victory or defeat for either system.... Command economies have the power to jump-start large scale industrialization, but they are unable to maximize efficiency. Such countries expand economically by making huge investments in productive capacity, but they cannot produce efficiently enough to compete with those of the Western industrialized world.

The authoritarian regime in South Korea also achieved spectacular growth rates by practicing command economics. This fact flies in the face of conventional development dogma. Government incentives, subsidies, and coercion fueled the drive for heavy industry in such areas as iron and steel that market forces would have rendered uncompetitive in the early stages. These sectors then built up the infrastructure South Korea needed to become a world-class exporter of such higher value-added goods as cars and VCRs.

South Korea's technocrats enlarged the application of market principles in the early 1980s, whereas the East European economies failed to do so. The South Korean economy's resumption of growth after a brief period of stagnation at the onset of the 1980s and Eastern Europe's slowdown after rapid growth in the 1960s confirms a more complex truth than that purveyed by free-market ideologues: Command economies may propel societies through the first stages of development, but further growth into a more sophisticated economy necessitates a greater role for market mechanisms, albeit with guidance from the state.

At the same time, there should be no illusions about the adverse consequences of market mechanisms on equity. Both China and Vietnam, for example, have increased agricultural output by freeing market forces. Yet both countries have experienced growing inequalities. While some farmers are getting richer, some consumers are going hungry in the face of rising food prices. Post-1978 economic reforms in China have increased income inequalities in both urban and rural areas.[8]

Other lessons emerge from Eastern Europe and the socialist developing world. While some of these countries did perform redistributive reforms, providing significant health and education services, they, like the NICs, have failed in the realms of ecological sustainability and political participation. Indeed, proponents of the free market fail to address a common demand coming from the citizens of China, Eastern Europe, South Korea, and Taiwan: Free markets are not a panacea; the average citizen must participate in decision making that affects his or her life.

Most developing countries, however, fall neither into the category of the NICs nor into the socialist world. For the development establishment, the lesson drawn from the experience of the NICs and the socialist countries is that developing countries' only hope rests with exporting their way to NIC status through the purgatory of structural adjustment. Dozens of countries across Africa, Asia, and Latin America have been force-fed this harsh prescription.

Supervised by the World Bank and the International Monetary Fund (IMF), these adjustment packages mandate severely cutting government spending to balance budgets, eliminating trade barriers and social subsidies, encouraging exports, tightening money policies, devaluing currencies, and dismantling nationalist barriers to foreign investment.

As we saw in Chapter 2, part of the West's sense of triumph flows from a feeling that a worldwide consensus has developed about the necessity of these reforms.[9] But many Western development authorities ignore the fact that the so-called Washington Consensus has been pushed on developing-country governments with a heavy hand. After borrowing sprees in the 1970s, most developing countries ran into debt-servicing difficulties in the 1980s. Creditor banks, using the World Bank and IMF as enforcers, conditioned debt rescheduling on acceptance of export-oriented structural adjustment packages. In fact, many poorer countries faced serious external constraints on export opportunities—from growing protectionism in developed-country markets to increased substitution for raw-material exports.

The Failures of Structural Adjustment

The strategy urged on poorer nations suffers from other shortcomings as well. Structural adjustment in practice has damaged environments, worsened structural inequities, failed even in the very narrow goal of pulling economies forward, and bypassed popular participation. Now many of the democratic movements expanding across the globe are rejecting the profoundly undemocratic approach of neoliberalism.

Ecological sustainability has been undermined in country after country. In their frenzy to export, countries often resort to the easiest short-term approach: unsustainable exploitation of natural resources. The stories of ecological disasters lurking behind export successes have become common: Timber exporting has denuded mountains, causing soil erosion and drying critical watersheds. Forests were cleared, for example, as Costa Rica, encouraged by the World Bank, expanded cattle production for meat exports, and as Indonesia expanded palm oil production.[10]

Cash crop exports have depended on polluting pesticides and fertilizers. Large fishing boats have destroyed the coral reefs in which fish breed and live. Tailings from mines have polluted rivers and bays. And, with the widespread destruction of natural-resource systems, the very survival of the poorest populations of these countries, those who live off the natural resources, has been threatened.

Workers too have paid a heavy price as their governments were encouraged to offer tax and other incentives to woo foreign investment. As a result, factories exporting apparel, electronics, toys, and other consumer goods sprang up in southern China, Vietnam, Guatemala, Malaysia, and dozens of other countries. Yet, even as countries compete with each other for foreign investment, in what critics have dubbed a "race to the bottom," workers in most of the new global factories in poorer nations are underpaid, overworked, and denied fundamental rights, including the right to organize and strike, and the right to a safe working environment.

Structural adjustment hurts the poor in other ways, too. As government spending is reduced, social programs are decimated. One May 1989 World Bank working paper concluded that a by-product of the "sharply deteriorating social indicators" that accompany contractionary adjustment packages is that "people below the poverty line will probably suffer irreparable damage in health, nutrition, and education."[11] Another World Bank working paper, published in September 1989, on Costa Rica, El Salvador, and Haiti, suggested that the concentration of land in the hands of a few, along with population growth, was a major cause of environmental degradation.[12] Skewed land distribution, it argued, pushed marginalized peasants onto fragile ecosystems. However, as the report noted, the adjustment programs in these countries failed to address distributional issues, focusing instead on correcting "distorted prices." In this regard, Taiwan and South Korea offer historical precedents: Their economic success rested on an initial redistribution of the land. Although some agricultural policies have been biased against the peasantry, extensive land reforms in the 1950s helped create the internal market that sustained the early stages of industrialization.

The failures of structural adjustment in the areas of environment and equity might appear less serious if the adjustment packages were scoring economic successes. They, however, are not. The first World Bank structural adjustment loans were given to Kenya, the Philippines, and Turkey in the early 1980s. A decade later, none can be rated a success story. A UN Economic Commission for Africa study has highlighted the World Bank's own findings that after structural adjustment programs, fifteen African countries were worse off in a number of economic categories.[13]

The lesson of the 1980s teaches that there are no shortcuts to development. Development strategies will not succeed and endure unless they incorporate ecological sustainability, equity, and participation, as well as effectiveness in raising material living standards.

Countries focusing on any of these principles to the exclusion of others will probably fall short in the long run, if they have not already. The World Bank and the IMF, either by ignoring these first three principles in their structural adjustment reforms or, at best, by treating them as afterthoughts, have adjusted economies to the short-term benefit of narrow elite interests. Their fixation on high gross national product growth rates ensures that the costs in terms of people and resources will mount and overwhelm an economy at a later date, much as they have in South Korea and Taiwan.

People Power

While governmental approaches to development are failing across Africa, Asia, and Latin America, development initiatives are flourishing among citizens' organizations. Indeed, a natural relationship exists between the two levels. The failure of governments in development has given birth to many citizens' initiatives.

Popular organizations are taking on ecological destruction, inequitable control over resources and land, and governments' inability to advance the quality of life. And often the people are struggling in the face of government and military repression. Many citizens' groups are pushing for a central role in development—a concept they do not measure solely in terms of economic growth. At the core of almost all these movements lies an emphasis on participation of members in initiating and implementing plans, and in exercising control over their own lives. Hence, democracy becomes the central theme.

In the Philippines, according to our calculations, some five million people participate in citizens' groups.[14] Alan Durning of the Worldwatch Institute estimated that across the developing world more than 100 million people belong to hundreds of thousands of these organizations.[15] Official development organizations have difficulty taking these groups seriously and to date act as though they have little bearing on national development strategies. Our research suggests the opposite: The programs and experience of these grassroots groups will form the basis for new development strategies of the 1990s.

During the past decade, many of the most vibrant organizations have been born in battles over the destruction of natural resources. By the end of the 1980s, thousands of organizations across the developing world were campaigning against timber companies, unsustainable agriculture, industrial pollution, nuclear power plants, and the giant projects that many governments equate with development. In 1989, 60,000 indigenous people, landless laborers, and peasants gathered in a small town in India to protest a series of dams in the Narmada Valley to which the World Bank had committed $450 million.[16] On the other side of the world, indigenous Brazilians from forty tribal nations gathered that year to oppose construction of several hydroelectric dams planned for the Xingu River. Soon thereafter, indigenous people, rubber tappers, nut gatherers, and river people formed the Alliance of the Peoples of the Forest to Save the Amazon.[17]

In struggles over the control of resources, many also have ended up challenging powerful entrenched interests and inequitable structures. It is in this context that Philippine environmental leader Maximo "Junie" Kalaw succinctly encapsulated for us the root-cause of the struggle over Philippine forest resources: "In the past fifteen years we have had only 470 logging concessionaires who own all the resources of the forests. The process created poverty for seventeen million people around the forest areas."

In addition to ecology and equity, people's organizations have acted on the inability of governments to meet the most basic human needs and rights outlined in the UN's International Covenant on Economic, Social and Cultural Rights: the rights to "adequate food, clothing and housing." All over the world, informal economic institutions have sprung up to fill the economic void left by cuts in government spending. Development analysts Sheldon Annis and Peter Hakim have filled a book with examples of successful worker-owned businesses, transportation collectives, peasant leagues, micro-enterprise credit associations, and other citizen initiatives across Latin America.[18] Africa specialist Fantu Cheru refers to such groups in Africa as participants in a "silent revolution."[19]

Will the future see coalitions of citizens' organizations help elect governments with sustainable development agendas in Brazil, the Philippines, South Africa, and elsewhere—much as they ushered new governments into Eastern Europe in 1989? Even where citizens' coalitions do not take over the reins of state power, will these new, innovative groups be able to build links to segments of bureaucracies and even militaries that express openness to the sustainable development agenda?

Our research has uncovered positive signs in many countries. But a caveat is important: In order to gauge the success of these initiatives, one must shift away from exclusive interest in aggregate growth figures toward the more meaningful indicators of ecological sustainability, participation, equity, and quality of life for the poorer majority.

Beyond the sheer number of citizen initiatives that advance these indicators, a further measure of success revolves around the ability of local groups to form countrywide associations that address national issues. Over the past half-decade in the Philippines, for example, a coalition of dozens of peasant organizations representing 1.5 million members has gathered tens of thousands of signatures for a comprehensive and technically feasible national "People's Agrarian Reform Code." The code could become the centerpiece of a national development strategy in this predominantly agrarian country that suffers from an abysmal land-tenure situation.

As the peasant supporters of the People's Agrarian Reform Code lobby Congress for passage of their code, they are simultaneously taking steps to implement portions of the desperately needed reform on their own. A 1989 report documented fourteen representative cases around the country: actions by thousands of poor families to occupy 800 hectares of idle or abandoned lands, the seizure of idle fishponds, boycott of rent payments on land, spread of organic farming techniques, revival of traditional rice varieties, and the reforestation of mangroves in coastal areas.[20] In other African, Asian, and Latin American countries, coalitions of peasants, workers, women, and small entrepreneurs are banding together to craft policy alternatives.

Ultimately, the greatest successes in sustainable development will come when citizen groups elect their representatives into government. Governments that are more representative can help transform sustainable development initiatives into reality. Such governments can help build up an economic infrastructure and an internal market, create a network of social services, and set rules for a country's integration into the world economy. These three tenets do not represent another universal model to replace those of the market fundamentalists or of Marxist-Leninists: The past four decades are littered with the failures of universal models. However, the outlines of a more positive government role in development can be sketched using the principles of ecological sustainability, equity, participation, and effectiveness.

South Korea and Taiwan offer positive lessons for the ideal governmental role in the economy. The main lesson is not that the government should be taken out of the economy. Instead, the NICs' experiences suggest that success depends on governments standing above vested interests to help create the social and political infrastructure for economic growth. Indeed, though it may sound paradoxical, one needs an effective government to create the market.

The problem in many developing countries is not too much government, but a government that is too tangled in the web of narrow interest groups. The Philippine government, for example, serves as the private preserve of special economic interests. In South Korea, on the other hand, the weakness of the landed and business elite allowed the government to set the direction for development in the 1960s and 1970s. Without an assertive government that often acted against the wishes of international agencies and big business, South Korea would never have gained the foundation of heavy- and high-technology industries that enabled it to become a world-class exporter of high value–added commodities.

Placing governments above the control of economic interest groups presents no easy task in countries where a small number of powerful families control much of the land and resources. To increase the chances of success, strong citizens' groups must put their representatives in government, continue to closely monitor government actions, and press for redistributive reforms that weaken the power of special interests.

While independent governments can help push economies through the early stages of development, progress to more mature economies seems to require more market mechanisms to achieve effective production and distribution. For market mechanisms to work, however, there must first be a market. And for the majority of the developing world, creating a market with consumers possessing effective demand requires eliminating the severe inequalities that depress the purchasing power of workers and peasants. The "how to" list necessitates such steps as land reform, progressive taxation, and advancement of workers' rights.

Pragmatism is also essential for the integration of developing countries into the world economy. The choice facing these countries should not be viewed as an ideological one between import substitution and export-oriented growth, neither of which alone has generated sustainable development. Basing development on exports that prove to be ecologically damaging not only ignores sustainability, it fails to ask the more fundamental question of whom development should benefit. But building an export base on top of a strong internal market does make sense. In this scheme, foreign exchange receipts would shift from primary commodities to processed commodities, manufactures, and environmentally sensitive tourism. China, India, South Korea, and Taiwan all based their early industrial development on slowly raising the real incomes of their domestic populations. Each opened up to varying degrees to the world market and to foreign capital only after substantial domestic markets had been developed and nurtured.

Concerted citizen action can bring about more participatory, equitable, and ecologically sustainable development. At least one historical precedent can be cited, albeit on a subnational level: the postwar experience of Kerala, traditionally one of India's poorest states. With a population of 27 million, Kerala has more people than most developing countries. A long history of large movements by people of the lower castes culminated in the election of progressive state governments beginning in 1957. Constant pressure by India's most active agricultural labor unions and other peasant organizations forced these governments to abolish tenancy in what was one of the most sweeping agrarian reforms in South and Southeast Asia and place a high priority on health and literacy. In periods when conservative governments were voted into power in Kerala, the nongovernmental citizens' organizations remained strong enough to win reforms and ensure enforcement of existing laws. Despite income levels below the Indian average, Kerala boasts the highest life expectancy and literacy rates among Indian states, as well as the lowest infant mortality and birthrates.[21]

Kerala also highlights an important caveat: New, more accountable governments should not be seen as a panacea. Even popular governments cannot provide the answer to the wide array of development problems. No matter who wields state power, strong independent citizens' groups will continue to be central to sustainable development. Perhaps South Korea and Taiwan would be more successful societies if they had combined their early land reforms and thoughtful state intervention with a prolonged commitment to ecology, equity, and participation.

Democratic participation in the formulation and implementation of development plans forms the central factor in determining their medium- and long-term viability. This, however, is a controversial premise. Indeed, such a pronounced emphasis on democracy flies in the face of political scientist Samuel Huntington's claim in the 1960s that order must precede democracy in the early stages of development. Many still believe authoritarian governments in Eastern Europe, South Korea, and Taiwan served as the catalysts for industrialization that in turn created the conditions for advancing democracy.

Experiences of the last two decades suggest otherwise. Much of Africa, home to dozens of one-party authoritarian states, remains a development disaster. Argentina, Brazil, the Philippines, and other Asian and Latin American countries ruled by authoritarian governments have suffered similar fates. As political scientist Atul Kohli has documented, the economies of the relatively democratic regimes in Costa Rica, India, Malaysia, Sri Lanka, and Venezuela have "grown at moderate but steady rates" since the 1960s and income inequalities have "either remained stable or even narrowed."[22]

Moreover, in South Korea and Taiwan, authoritarian characteristics of the government were not responsible for industrialization and growth. Far-reaching land reforms and each state's ability to rise above factions in civil society deserve credit for sparking growth. The only "positive" growth impact of repression by these governments was to hold down wage levels, thereby making exports more competitive. Yet heavy dependence on exports no longer serves as an option in today's increasingly protectionist global markets. The percentage of imports into the major developed countries that were affected by nontariff barriers to trade rose more than 20 percent during the 1980s, a trend that is likely to continue. In this hostile global economic climate, respect for workers' rights can lead to the creation of local markets by increasing domestic buying power (we expand on this in Chapter 5). Democratic development therefore implies shifting emphasis from foreign to domestic (or, for small countries, to regional) markets. This shift meets more needs of local people and takes into account the difficult world market of the 1980s and 1990s.

The portrait painted at the outset—of a global development crisis masked by triumphant Western development orthodoxy—was a decidedly gloomy one. Why then should citizens' movements pushing for more equitable, sustainable, and participatory development stand a chance in the future? Much of the answer lies in the extraordinary possibilities of the current historical moment.

Development After the Cold War

For four decades, the Cold War has steered almost all development discussions toward ideological arguments over capitalism versus communism, market versus planning. It has also diverted public attention away from nonideological global concerns (such as environment, health, and economic decay) and toward the Soviet Union as the source of problems. Hence, the dramatic winding down of the Cold War opens great opportunities for development.[23]

At the very minimum, real debate should now become possible, getting beyond sharply drawn ideological categories in order to discuss development in more pragmatic terms. What are the proper roles of government and market? If one values both effectiveness and equity, what kind of checks should be placed on the market? What do the experiences of Japan, South Korea, and Taiwan bring to this discussion?

Rekindling the development debate requires listening to new approaches from the rest of the world. Excessive confidence in free-market approaches melts when one examines the mounting crises in the supposed success stories of South Korea and Taiwan. Exciting alternatives to neoliberalism are emerging in the hundreds of thousands of citizens' groups that flourish amid adversity and repression in Africa, Asia, and Latin America. These voices must be heard in the development establishments of Washington, Tokyo, and the capitals of Europe.

Chapter 4
_____

Myths About the Environment Strengthen

Our next stop is 1993—just a year after the world's largest-ever environmental summit was held in Rio de Janeiro. That so-called Earth Summit, officially the UN Conference on Environment and Development, was treated by many pundits and much of the media as a catalytic moment in global environmental awareness, as an event that reflected the awakening of the world to the fragile state of our planet.

However, as you glimpsed in the prior chapter and as you will witness in more detail in the current chapter, on the ground across the South the environment had already become both a focus and a symbol of what was wrong with neoliberal development efforts. Even without global summits and long before Al Gore made his climate-change movie and before even George Bush admitted to global warming, the environment had already become a spur to widespread local action by organized communities around the world. Moreover, this kind of local action on behalf of the environment presages what is to come through the entire alter-globalization movement—action taken not just on behalf of the environment but in relation to human-rights issues, labor issues, debt issues, and the whole ball of development wax.

Yet, as you will see in this chapter, more than a decade into the era of the Washington Consensus, the 1992 Earth Summit was a product of its time and did little to challenge the core myths that gave credence to the ever-spreading Consensus. Rather, quite the opposite: A new justification was added to neoliberalism, namely the erroneous notion that growth via "free trade" policies would help the environment. And, alas, the framing of the summit gave popularity to another vicious myth: That the poor were the key destroyers of the environment and that channeling aid to them for economic growth was the solution.

As in our 1990 time travel in Chapter 3, our perceptions were strongly influenced by what we had seen and heard through living with very ordinary people—poor farmers, fisher-folk, forest dwellers, and urban poor, among others. Bureaucrats who worked in financial institutions, governments, and aid agencies brought to the Earth Summit their perceptions that the poor were the chief culprits in environmental decay. Our experiences on the ground taught us the opposite: The poor can be the best defenders of forests, fishing grounds, and farm lands because their entire livelihood depends on these natural resources. Around the world, largely off camera, millions of poor people struggle daily to protect the environment from global corporations, local elites, and misguided aid projects. At the start of the 1990s, as today, the poor are central to the global backlash against market fundamentalism, and garnering local community control over natural resources is central to viable solutions to environmental destruction and to meaningful development.

As the curtain opens to Chapter 4 and 1993, we stand at the cusp of a moment of opportunity. Our travel unfolds not only against the backdrop of the Earth Summit but also the other defining event of 1992—the election of Bill Clinton and Al Gore in the United States. As we point out in this chapter, that election offered enormous opportunities to change course, to reexamine key tenets of neoliberalism. Clinton's campaign rhetoric suggested that he knew the Consensus was eroding labor and environmental rights and standards, and Gore's *Earth in the Balance* offered visionary alternatives. While we offer hope in the chapter that follows, we do so keenly aware of how deeply entrenched were the core precepts of the Consensus among economists, global corporations, the mainstream media, and key government leaders (including most of Clinton's and Gore's cabinet).

The key debate of the first two years of the Clinton administration was over the draft North American Free Trade Agreement (NAFTA), which it inherited from the first Bush administration. That agreement was sold with promises that freeing up trade and investment in North America would help workers and the environment in the United States, Canada, and Mexico. We were participants in the vibrant citizen networks that challenged NAFTA and that put forward bold alternatives for a just and sustainable North America. The battle over NAFTA was won by a hair by Washington Consensus backers in November 1993—and only after intense pressure and political maneuvering (de facto vote-buying).[1] While NAFTA passed and went into law, the arguments posed by its citizen opposition would frame the subsequent decade's development debates.

With that as your introduction, let us travel to 1993, looking at three core myths that defined the Earth Summit and the NAFTA debates, as well as emerging citizen blueprints for changing course.

⇥——⇤

1993—The administration of George H. W. Bush (1988–1992) has bequeathed to President Clinton two immediate Third World economic policy challenges of enormous importance to the United States: a deeply flawed trade agreement with our North American neighbors and a beleaguered and ineffectual foreign-aid establishment. The Clinton/Gore administration's response to these trade and aid challenges is vital as much for domestic reasons as for what they portend for the poorer four-fifths of the globe. The U.S. economy is so interwoven with that of Mexico and other poorer nations that their well-being affects the quantity and quality of our jobs, the fate of our environment, and the viability of any new economic program that President Clinton initiates.

No gathering crystallized new public understandings of these global interconnections better than the 1992 United Nations Earth Summit in Rio de Janeiro. With the Senate's leading environmental advocate—Gore—emerging as a potentially powerful U.S. vice president, there is the opportunity to harness the Earth Summit's consciousness-raising to help reshape U.S. policy toward the developing world.

Pitfalls, however, abound. For even as the Earth Summit opened eyes to the need for new North–South discussions, it perpetuated myths about who is to blame for the problems and what steps to take. Three overriding myths pervaded the Earth Summit debates and permeate the Bush administration trade and aid policies inherited by the new president:

- *The Poor Are the Problem:* The most prevalent myth is that only rich people in rich countries have the luxury to care about the environment. Poor people in poor countries must focus on survival. And in so doing, the rapidly expanding ranks of poorer people in developing countries have become the main culprit behind environmental destruction.
- *Growth Will Resolve Environmental Problems:* Building on the first myth, many contend that the key to stemming poverty and slowing environmental destruction in poorer countries is stimulating growth by better integrating poor countries into the world market. Such growth, it is said, will not only relieve the environmentally destructive poverty, it

will also generate the financial means to solve environmental problems.

- *Aid Is the Answer:* A third myth delineates the North–South relationship. If Northerners want officials in poor countries to share their
environmental concerns, there must be a massive increase in aid from
wealthier countries, such as the United States, to pay for the environment and development initiatives discussed at Rio.

Judging from early appointments, the new administration contains an un-
wieldy mix of myth believers and myth challengers. Vice President Al Gore,
in his writings and speeches, has confronted some of these myths. Yet at the
helm of the executive branch's most potent economic agency, the Treasury
Department, is former senator Lloyd Bentsen, one of the major supporters
of the Bush free-trade agreements. And his undersecretary in the powerful
international slot is another true myth believer, former World Bank chief
economist Lawrence Summers. If the latter forces dominate the administration's debates, their perpetuation of the myths threatens to steer U.S. policy
toward a series of well-meaning but disastrous aid and trade programs.

Are the Poor the Problem?

By the end of the Earth Summit, many participants and journalists were
articulating a simple equation to explain the complex relationship between
environment and development: Poverty causes environmental degradation.
They portrayed rich countries and wealthy people as environmentalists
pressing for curbs on tropical deforestation to combat global climate change.
They saw developing countries and poor people as fixated on survival and
basic development issues—and if exploitation of natural resources contributed to those goals, so be it.

We have posed this rich-poor, North-South dichotomy to a number
of people from organizations of small-scale farmers, fishers, and miners in
developing countries. Their responses are instructive: Poor people in poor
countries may not have heard of global warming or ozone depletion, but
their local ecological crises have often forced them to act in defense of the
environment.

Consider but one example. On a hot, dusty day in the late 1980s, several
dozen poor peasants in the southern Philippines sat down in the middle
of the narrow dirt road that runs from logging camps in the mountains
above, through their town, to the sawmills of the town below. Holding
hand-lettered signs that read "LOGGERS STOP!", they proceeded to

make "citizens' arrests" of logging trucks. For nearly two weeks, they slept, ate, and held mass on that road until they had blockaded more than thirty logging trucks.

These people sat down to save their lands. As one explained, without the trees whose roots serve as sponges to store water and anchor soil, typhoon rains rush down the bare slopes and wash away precious topsoil. "Without trees," she told us, "there is no food, and without food, no life." The point here is not simply that they acted; they persevered against government lethargy, corruption, and connivance with the powerful commercial logging interests in the area.[2]

This action highlights one weakness in the conventional Rio analysis of the North-South dichotomy: Everyone in the South is considered to have the same interests—government, business, and the majority of poorer rural and urban dwellers. It assumes that governments stand above vested interests to represent broadly shared concerns in the pursuit of societal development.

The reality, however, is often quite different. A small number of families in Brazil, Honduras, Zaire, Indonesia, and many other countries control economic and political power and use government power for private enrichment. And in natural-resource-rich countries, the quickest route to wealth is frequently through maximum exploitation of land, minerals, forests, and marine resources. In these countries, the overlapping interests and identities of politicians and business people—commercial logging companies owned by congressional representatives, presidential relatives, and retired military officers—make for powerful lobbies in favor of continued exploitation.

In other words, given this political economy of natural-resource degradation, the poor do not cause most environmental problems; the rich do. It is therefore not surprising that governmental representatives from such countries do not consider environmental concerns to be primary. We do not dispute that poor people under desperate conditions often contribute individually to environmental degradation through rapid population growth and migration to fragile ecosystems, or that most countries need more effective voluntary family-planning programs. But to view poverty as the root cause is to miss the dynamic of inequality and powerlessness. For instance, it is the rich loggers whose roads open up the forest to the poorer settlers; the loggers' vast forest holdings contribute to the grossly inequitable land-distribution patterns typical of natural-resource-rich countries. In Brazil, for example, many of those poor, shifting agriculturalists who are blamed for Amazonian deforestation have actually been pushed off their small farms in southern Brazil by agri-businessmen who are expanding their soybean plantations for a profitable export market.

On the other hand, to understand why it is the poor who are more likely to become environmentalists in developing countries, often facing off against the rich, one has to appreciate that the majority of environmental problems there involve the depletion and degradation of natural resources at the start of the production chain. Forests and fishing grounds, for most people in the South, are sources of livelihood, not places for recreation. This concern is quite different from the air and water pollution and waste-disposal problems that most city-dwellers and Northern citizens think of as ecological challenges.

Throughout the developing world, poor people motivated by survival are fighting back. Poor Filipino farmers are rejecting the Green Revolution seeds that indebt them to pesticide and fertilizer companies and, instead, are planting traditional rice varieties that do not require chemical inputs. Women in Kenya and Mozambique have organized "greenbelt movements" to reclaim parts of cities for vegetable gardens and to experiment with sustainable agroforestry techniques. Indigenous people, rubber tappers, nut gatherers, and river people from across Brazil have united in an alliance to save the Amazon.

To these grassroots environmentalists, the key question is the one posed by Indian ecologist Vandana Shiva: "Who protects which environment from whom?"[3] Or as one Philippine environmental leader explains to us: "Democratizing control of resources is the key to sustainable development." Indeed, the emerging environmental movement in the Philippines, as in Malaysia, Indonesia, Brazil, Kenya, and elsewhere, is a struggle for equitable control and management of natural resources.

The success or failure of any new U.S. initiatives to prevent further environmental degradation in the South depends on the U.S. government and citizens' groups collaborating with organizations of poorer people. For the poor are often not only the catalysts for halting the destruction, they are also the initiators of sustainable and equitable alternatives.

Is Free-Market Growth the Solution?

Myths beget more myths. If poor people and Southern countries are viewed as too poor to care about the environment, then poverty must be attacked through economic growth and by siphoning off some of the growing financial resources to clean up the environment. According to conventional wisdom in aid and development circles, the path toward such growth is to unleash market forces. This means ending trade restrictions, cutting government subsidies, and privatizing state enterprises—all "market distortions" that, it is argued, also provoke environmental degradation. As the Rio Declaration on Environment and Development, signed by governments at the Earth Summit, says: "States should cooperate to promote a supportive and open international economic system that would lead to economic growth and sustainable development ... to better address the problems of environmental degradation."

Princeton economists Alan Krueger and Gene Grossman are often-cited promoters of this argument. Their 1992 study concluded that when countries pass the threshold of $4,000–$5,000 in per capita gross domestic product, emissions of three specific air pollutants tend to decrease. In a *New York Times* opinion piece, Grossman suggested that one could, from this finding, conclude that "attention to environmental issues is a luxury poor countries cannot afford. Once a country is able to feed its people, it begins to be willing to pay the costs of controlling pollution and cleaning up problems."[4] In other words, as then World Bank chief economist Lawrence Summers claimed: "Growth creates both the way and the will to improve the environment."[5]

This argument, which has been labeled an "environmental Kuznets curve," is specious for a number of reasons. It confuses government and elite interests with those of the poorer majority. Environmental issues, as we have seen, are anything but a luxury for the many who need resources to survive. Further, as Vice President Gore has argued in the case of the United States, economic activity can either help sustain the environment or it can deplete resources, pollute, and destroy the environment. Just as investment in mass transit, energy conservation, and green technology can create U.S. jobs in a more environmentally sound fashion, alternative energy, regenerative agriculture, and sustainable fishing practices can do the same in the developing world.

Firms operating in free markets, however, tend to promote virulent strains of environmentally destructive growth. In an age of global economic integration, the kind of growth that is being encouraged in both the North and South is one where companies and countries compete by cutting costs anywhere they can. Wages and environmental standards are prime areas for such cuts. Consider Mexico's willingness to be lax in environmental enforcement as an enticement to new investment along the U.S.-Mexican border—an area that unregulated corporate expansion has transformed into what the American Medical Association calls "a virtual cesspool and breeding ground for infectious disease."[6] The U.S. General Accounting Office conducted a random sampling of twelve U.S. companies operating in Mexico and confirmed that all twelve were out of compliance with Mexico's environmental requirements. In other words, Mexico's strategy of growth is based on competing in global markets through violations of labor and environmental standards.

Finally, market-based growth strategies that do not address the extreme inequalities of wealth and resource ownership across the developing world not only make no environmental sense, they also make no economic sense in the medium- to long-term. The fact that so few have access to land and other resources and that unregulated global competition keeps wages low means that there are extreme limits on the creation of markets in much of the developing world. And, in the end, if only 10 to 20 percent of a country's population can purchase the goods that country produces, then prospects for broad-based development are dim indeed.

The key issue is still who controls the resources. "You cannot have a technical solution without addressing access to resources," explains Chip Fay, former Friends of the Earth representative to Asia. "Investing into the existing resource-allocation system is investing in a structure that is unsustainable." The only way out is to break the connection between the politicians and the resource controllers, a feat that—once again—requires democratizing control of resources.

Is Aid the Answer?

A final myth—that more aid is necessary—follows the well-established tradition of calling for a modern–day Marshall Plan to solve whatever international problem the world faces. The *Washington Post* summed up the Earth Summit in an editorial that proposed: "If they want the [poorer countries] not to struggle laboriously through the slash-and-burn, coal-and-sulfur stages of development, the rich are going to have to provide them with the resources to bypass it. That means money and technology."[7] In this spirit, Earth Summit chairman Maurice Strong spent a great deal of time before and after the summit pleading for billions of dollars in new aid.

We need to understand the Marshall Plan for what it was: the very exceptional case where throwing money at a problem actually worked because the task was *rebuilding* physical infrastructure in highly industrialized societies ravaged by war. To assume that massive aid inflows, coursing through the multilateral development banks and such bilateral institutions as the U.S. Agency for International Development, can solve the South's environmental problems is to ignore decades of documentation demonstrating that such aid has actually *compounded* the environmental degradation.[8] And, as the Brazilian environmentalist and one-time top government environmental official, Jose Lutzenberger, has argued, giving these institutions more money to lend would simply encourage them to fund larger projects—an environmentalist's nightmare, since the history of mega-projects is one of mega-disasters.

In the last decade, a number of environmental and development groups in the North and South have launched politically sophisticated campaigns to confront the World Bank.[9] As a result, the World Bank now talks a greener line, has its own environment department, and requires environmental assessments of those projects it deems to have potential environmental impact. But there is little evidence that the Bank has lived up to its new rhetoric. The overarching neoliberal "structural adjustment" framework it imposes on poor countries does not undergo environmental impact assessments— and still centers on policy shifts to encourage exports and cut government spending, shifts that are often environmentally destructive. And there are still too many giant aid projects, such as the highly controversial dams that are displacing entire communities in Thailand, Argentina, and India.

Once again, the bottom line remains the same: The history of aid suggests that its success depends on getting it to the right people. To stimulate environmentally beneficial programs, we need to get smaller amounts of aid to organizations of the poor that are committed to equitable and participatory development. We need not more aid, but less and better aid.

Transforming the North's Policies

By accepting these myths about growth, aid, and the poor, negotiators at the Earth Summit conveniently avoided two of the central barriers to reversing environmental degradation across the planet: the widespread inequalities that characterize natural-resource ownership in much of the world, and the environmentally destructive tendencies of large corporations in a deregulated world economy. For its part, the Clinton/Gore administration can begin transforming the North's policies by rethinking free-trade and investment agreements, particularly the North American Free Trade Agreement (NAFTA), and overhauling U.S. foreign assistance as channeled through multilateral institutions and the widely criticized U.S. Agency for International Development.

Unlike Earth Summit declarations, trade agreements can include binding mechanisms with the power of trade sanctions to enforce environmental standards. This is where the Clinton/Gore administration can confront the environmentally and socially destructive consequences of economic integration. The first opportunity is with what George Bush counts as among his greatest presidential accomplishments—NAFTA, which will eliminate trade barriers and lower investment barriers among the three economies of the continent. During the campaign period, candidate Clinton said that he would send this agreement to Congress only after supplemental agreements were negotiated on labor and environmental issues.

Here is the challenge: So long as U.S. firms can pour toxic waste into the Mexican soil and violate the basic rights of Mexican workers, Mexico will be a magnet for runaway shops. Moreover, U.S.-based firms will use the threat of moving across the Rio Grande to bargain down conditions here. The solution is not protectionism but rather defining the kind of integration and globalization we want and using trade agreements to promote that end. In order to rebuild our domestic economy in an era when U.S. corporations are global, it is in our collective interest to help pull up environmental, working, and living standards in Mexico and the rest of the developing world. Therefore, an agreement with Mexico, along with any other regional trade agreements we negotiate, must incorporate binding environmental and labor rights and standards. So too with the ongoing negotiations to create a World Trade Organization. Violations of the rights and standards should be treated like any other unfair trade practice; the violators should lose the benefits of freer trade.

For NAFTA, the political constituencies for such positions already exist. Environmental, labor, farm, and development groups from Mexico, Canada, and the United States have sketched the outlines of such a just and workable policy framework, building on labor rights and standards that are already part of U.S. trade law.[10] And, in fact, Vice President Gore endorsed this approach in *Earth in the Balance:* "Just as government subsidies of a particular industry are sometimes considered unfair under the trade laws, weak and ineffectual enforcement of pollution control measures should also be included in the definition of unfair trading practices."[11] He and President Clinton have the opportunity to put this idea into practice as they reconsider NAFTA and as they take over the negotiations to replace the General Agreement on Tariffs and Trade (GATT) with a World Trade Organization.

Redefining Aid

Beyond trade, the U.S. administration can also begin to redefine the meaning of aid, so as to help build a new partnership with the poorer nations of the world. As we have said, the dilemma here is how to get more out of less.

If President Clinton studies the current uses of aid, he will discover that most of it is actually given as loans and often exacerbates the developing world's already staggering debt burden. Even loans for environmental projects can backfire in this way, as Ford Foundation official Frances Korten has pointed out: "Environmental loans ... must be repaid, creating pressures for exports. The options developing countries face for generating foreign revenues are limited and many involve ecologically damaging exploitation of natural resources."[12] Twelve years of Republican administrations have blocked any global efforts to reduce the over one-trillion dollars—and growing—debt of the developing world; the Clinton/Gore administration would do well to take leadership in initiating such discussions on a global scale.

In getting more out of the economic and development funds, the U.S. administration faces two sets of institutions in need of reform: global lending institutions and the U.S. bilateral lending agency.

As to the first, the U.S. government must work with other donor and borrower countries to insist not only that the World Bank base its lending on equitable and sustainable practices, but also that Bank projects incorporate meaningful public participation in design and implementation through regular consultation with organizations of the poor, women, peasants, workers, and others in affected areas.

As to the second, the U.S. government should set an example by redefining the mission and vision of its own lending agency. Aid should be delinked from the vestiges of Cold War strategic alliances, and security assistance should be phased out. If the most effective way to slow environmental degradation in poorer countries is to democratize control of resources so that communities can manage them more sustainably, we must ask how U.S. bilateral aid can help that process. The goal is clear: getting smaller amounts of aid—grants, not loans—to organizations of the poor that are committed to more equitable and participatory development.

Viable plans already exist. The Development Group for Alternative Policies along with fifteen other U.S. citizen groups, in consultation with partners in the developing world, crafted "The Development Cooperation Act" in 1990.[13] The act encouraged this type of assistance and spelled out guidelines to ensure "consultation with the poor at all stages of the development process" and new mechanisms to get aid directly to women, the landless, subsistence producers, migrants, and others who need it most and can use it best. Now is the moment to debate, refine, and implement such an act.

But more exists than simply plans on paper. There have been experiments in getting aid in smaller amounts directly to citizens' organizations. In the Philippines, thanks to the openness of some within the U.S. Congress and the creative vision and coordinated lobbying efforts of citizens' groups in the Philippines and the United States, $25 million in U.S. aid funds was approved to endow the Foundation for the Philippine Environment through a debt-for-nature swap. Based in Manila, the foundation is run by a board composed primarily of leaders of the Philippine sustainable-development movement. The board approves small grants to nongovernmental organizations, communities, and training institutions to fund new experiments in natural-resource preservation, community management of natural resources, and education and advocacy on the environment.

We can also learn a great deal from other nations, such as the Netherlands, Canada, and Australia, that have made small amounts of aid money go a long way. The Dutch government specifically targets its aid on poverty alleviation. It disburses up to a tenth of its aid through Dutch agencies that fund grassroots development initiatives directed at the poor. Part of this aid pays for education and training of individuals in citizens' organizations in order to increase the participation of people in the development process. Likewise, a share of Canadian and Australian aid funds sustainable-development programs that are designed by Canadian and Australian citizens' groups in collaboration with nongovernment groups in the recipient countries. These innovative programs have incorporated into projects the active involvement of women, sound ecological practices, and advocacy for human rights. They offer rich lessons for new U.S. initiatives in other countries.

The challenge to the new U.S. administration is to discard the myths that governed past administrations' policies and, instead, to assert leadership in negotiating new rules that address the ecological and social disintegration accompanying world economic integration. Here, and in reconceptualizing U.S. foreign-aid programs, a new U.S. administration has the bully pulpit to help Americans understand that in a global economy our real interests are best served by the promotion of equitable and sustainable development in the rest of the world.

Chapter 5

The North-South Divide Widens

We next touch ground almost halfway through U.S. president Bill Clinton's two terms and fifteen years into the reign of the Washington Consensus. It is a moment in time that speaks volumes to both the persistence and the adaptability of neoliberalism. Contrary to popular assumptions that the Republican Party is the main party of big business and contrary to our urgings in the last chapter, Clinton's Democratic administration embraced the Washington Consensus and sold it domestically as being good for U.S. business interests overseas and hence good for the United States.

With such U.S. business interests in mind, Clinton's Commerce Department termed key NICs and would-be NICs the "Big Emerging Markets" and encouraged those countries to welcome more U.S. trade and investment as they further liberalized their economies.

We view this shift through the multifaceted development lens we have acquired in our decade and a half of analyzing the Washington Consensus in action, and we find ourselves deeply troubled. What about the impact of this market-opening on the poorer majority and the environment in these ten to twelve countries? What about the majority of poorer countries who are not "big" or "emerging" in the U.S. government's view?

What we discover augments our overarching critique (raised in earlier chapters) of the flawed North-South framework that guides U.S. relations with the developing world. We argued then (as we do now) that corporate-led globalization policies largely benefited the wealthier majority in rich countries and a very rich minority in poor countries while hurting working families and the poor in both richer (North) and poorer (South) countries, resulting in what could be termed a global economic apartheid. As such, our analysis in the chapter you are about to read challenges the entire framework of the dominant development paradigm and suggests a very different way forward.

In 1995, however, the power of market fundamentalism was still strong. As you will witness in our travel to that time, the Consensus steamroller had changed the contours of development policy and practice across the globe. Its backers successfully accelerated corporate-friendly globalization rules, leading to the North American Free Trade Agreement (NAFTA) in 1994 and the World Trade Organization (WTO) in 1995. Each victory whetted the appetite of Consensus backers for more.

A case in point of "more" was financial liberalization: The IMF and World Bank, in tandem with the U.S. Treasury Department, essentially expanded the Consensus from trade liberalization to encompass capital liberalization, including ending restrictions on short-term, speculative financial flows. From our 1995 perch, we warn that crises stood on the horizon if poorer nations opened up too quickly and too widely to such "portfolio investment." In a later chapter (Chapter 6), we will see that exactly such a crisis erupted in Thailand in the summer of 1997 and spread like wildfire across the globe.

Lights, cameras, action . . .

—————

1995—For four and a half decades, the Cold War offered Americans a prism through which to view the three-quarters of humanity who live in the impoverished countries of Latin America, Africa, and Asia. The United States fought or funded wars and covert operations in dozens of these countries—including Cuba, the Dominican Republic, Guatemala, Iran, Korea, Nicaragua, and Vietnam—with the stated goal of preventing the spread of Soviet-backed communism. Shaped to meet this goal, U.S. economic and military policies toward the so-called Third World, or South, were relatively simple and straightforward.

In the mid-1990s, a half-decade into the confusing post–Cold War era and more than halfway through President Bill Clinton's first term, the Third World still erupts into the forefront of U.S. foreign policy with alarming regularity. The administration and media tend to categorize these episodes into one of three oversimplified images. The first and dominant one can be termed "the Rwanda image," and includes countries where, the media tells us, everything is falling apart, and people kill one another in large numbers. Bosnia in 1995, Haiti in 1994, and Somalia in 1993 fit the bill. A second image, promoted by beleaguered defense contractors and Pentagon hawks, paints certain volatile Third World nations and the former Soviet Union as emerging security threats equal to that posed by Moscow at the height of the Cold War. Here, North Korea and Iraq stand out, each with leaders easily caricatured by the media as Hollywood villains. Finally, there is the newer image of a financially tattered Mexico and the fear that other nations may plunge rapidly into similar crises; tens of billions of dollars of short-term speculative capital race around the globe, abandoning yesterday's favorite "emerging market" for promises of quick returns elsewhere.

Content to respond to crises in these three categories, the Clinton administration has yet to forge an overarching policy framework that addresses the deep and changing problems of the South, which comprises approximately 150 countries. In fact, aside from attention to some crisis spots, the administration forfeited the chance to craft a new North-South policy agenda, as we argued in Chapter 4. Instead, it preferred one that places in the foreground only a handful of these countries. And this policy is being managed not by the State or Treasury Department, but by the Commerce Department, which has singled out about ten promising "big emerging markets" for U.S. exports and investments.[1]

When pressed to articulate themes or values that underlie U.S. policy toward these countries and the rest of the South, Clinton administration officials unite around the rhetoric of markets and democracy: Freer markets, through such pacts as the North American Free Trade Agreement (NAFTA), will, they claim, bring both greater economic growth and greater democracy. Remarkably, the positions of most Republican leaders in Congress differ only slightly in substance from this agenda. They support the free-trade agenda and the notion that U.S. foreign policy should support U.S. business. A vocal minority who are more protectionist includes the powerful chairman of the Senate Foreign Relations Committee, Jesse Helms (R-NC). Despite his dramatic overstatements and misstatements that seek to distance him from the Democrats, Helms's attack on Clinton's North-South agenda has concentrated on one issue: cutting U.S. aid drastically (much of which, he likes to say, is "going down foreign rat-holes").[2]

Thus, Washington is poised to continue neglecting the South, except in response to crisis-based chaos or through free-trade agreements and business promotion aimed at a few Third World countries. This lack of a broader North-South economic agenda, however, may well turn out to be one of the great blunders of the Clinton administration. The danger of neglect lies beneath the facile surface images of the Third World reality: a deteriorating living standard for the poorest 2.5 billion people in the world, widening inequalities in almost every nation on earth, and employment and environmental crises that beg global initiatives.

The Clinton administration and the Republican Congress face three immediate opportunities to address these larger problems—opportunities that should be seized to frame a more comprehensive policy toward the South. First, the administration has begun considering the expansion of NAFTA to include the Caribbean Basin, Chile, and the rest of Latin America. Second, Congress is debating new criteria for giving U.S. aid to poor countries. And finally, Mexico's 1994–1995 footloose capital debacle initiated a propitious international deliberation on fundamental reform of the world's leading multilateral institutions—the World Bank and the International Monetary Fund (IMF)—to meet the new financial crises of the twenty-first century.

What is required to seize these opportunities is a deeper understanding of the new dynamics between North and South and a more comprehensive policy agenda. Unfortunately, Clinton's narrow policies are based on three deeply flawed assumptions (also shared by most Republican leaders) about the nature of the changes in the global economy.

The first incorrect assumption is that free trade and the promotion of U.S. business interests overseas are good for U.S. workers and communities. The U.S. Commerce Department is the clearest articulator of this view; it brought planeloads of corporate CEOs on trips to such "big emerging markets" as Brazil, China, and Indonesia. These trips and the two major free-trade agreements completed under Clinton—NAFTA and the World Trade Organization (WTO)—have offered tens of billions of dollars in new business overseas to the United States's largest firms. As the former deputy director of policy planning at the State Department, John Stremlau, wrote: The administration's big-emerging-markets program "should create millions of new and better-paying jobs for Americans, spur domestic productivity, ease adjustment to technological change, restrain inflation, and reduce trade and fiscal deficits."[3]

The second flawed assumption of U.S. policy is that free trade and increased U.S. engagement in the ten biggest emerging markets will not only help these economies but will also enhance growth in other Southern countries. Jumping on the big-emerging-markets bandwagon, American CEOs echo administration claims that U.S. policies are leading to the growth of huge middle classes—in such countries as China, India, and Indonesia—that will drive the world economy in the twenty-first century.

A third assumption is that the economic gap between rich and poor countries is now narrowing—a trend that the administration claims is aided by free trade and attention to the ten Third World countries with big emerging markets. Indeed, there is a widespread perception among U.S. policymakers that the Third World debt crisis that widened the gap during the 1980s has ended, that new capital is flowing into the Third World, and that the gap is beginning to close. These perceptions are reinforced by World Bank projections that over the next decade, Third World countries will actually grow faster than richer countries, thus catching up.[4]

Our careful analysis of social and economic data from the United Nations, the World Bank, the IMF, and other sources, offers a shockingly different picture of trends in the global economy and the gap between rich and poor countries. There are two ways to measure what is happening economically between North and South. The first is to measure which is growing faster, and therefore whether the gap between them is growing or shrinking. The second is to measure financial resource flows between the two.

On the first issue the picture is clear: The North-South gap widened dramatically in the decade after 1982 as the Third World debt crisis drained financial resources from poor countries to rich banks. Between 1985 and 1992, Southern nations paid some $280 billion more in debt-service to Northern creditors than they received in new private loans and government aid.[5] Gross national product (GNP) per capita rose an average of only 1 percent in the South in the 1980s (in sub-Saharan Africa, it fell 1.2 percent), while it rose 23 percent in the North.[6]

Situating the "lost decade" of the 1980s within a longer time period reveals no drastic change: In 1960, per capita gross domestic product (GDP) in the South stood at 18 percent of the average of Northern nations; by 1990, it had fallen only slightly to 17 percent.[7] In other words, the North-South gap remained fairly constant.

However, such aggregate figures camouflage a complex reality: For a small group of countries, primarily such big Asian emerging markets as China, Hong Kong, Singapore, South Korea, and Taiwan, the gap with the North has been closing. But—and here is the rub—for most of the rest, the gap has been slowly widening. In sub-Saharan Africa the picture is even worse. Not only has the gap expanded significantly, but for many of these countries, per capita GNP has continued to fall.[8]

Likewise, a look at various resource flows between North and South reveals a reality out of sync with prevailing assumptions. Despite the perception of an easing of the debt crisis, the overall Third World debt stock continues to swell by almost $100 billion each year (it reached $1.9 trillion in 1994).[9] Southern debt service still exceeds new lending, and the net outflow remains particularly crushing in Africa. While it is true that a series of debt reschedulings and the accumulation of arrears by many debtors have reduced the net negative financial transfer from South to North over the last few years, the flows remain negative.

Part of the reason some analysts argue that the debt crisis is no longer a problem is that since the early 1990s these outflows of debt repayments have been matched by increased inflows of foreign capital. Here too, however, a deeper look at disaggregated figures reinforces the disconcerting reality. According to World Bank figures, roughly half of the new foreign direct investment by global corporations in the South in 1992 quickly left those countries as profits.[10] In addition, investment flows primarily to only ten to twelve Third World countries that are viewed as new profit centers by Northern corporations and investors. More than 70 percent of investment in 1991 and 1992 went to just ten of the so-called emerging markets: Mexico, followed by China, Malaysia, Argentina, Thailand, Brazil, Indonesia, Venezuela, South Korea, and Turkey.[11]

There is another problem with these capital flows. Several of these countries (Brazil, India, Mexico, South Korea, and Taiwan) have attracted substantial short-term flows by opening their stock markets to foreigners and by issuing billions of dollars in bonds.[12] Between 1991 and 1993 alone, foreign direct investment as a share of all private capital flows into poor countries fell from 65 to 44 percent as these more speculative flows increased.[13] Events in Mexico provide an indication of the fickleness of these new investment flows: During the last week of 1994, an estimated $10 billion in short-term funds fled the country.[14]

In addition, Third World countries have been hurt by the declining buying power of their exports vis-a-vis their imports. Southern governments and other critics of neoliberalsim have long pointed out the general tendency of the prices of their primary product exports to rise more slowly than the prices of manufactured goods imports. This "terms of trade" decline was particularly sharp between 1985 and 1993 when the real prices of primary commodities fell 30 percent.[15] This translates into billions of dollars: The 3.5 percent decline in the purchasing power of Africa's 1993 exports, for example, cost the continent some $3 billion.[16]

The inescapable conclusion is that the North-South economic gap is narrowing for about a dozen countries but continues to widen for well over 100 others. Hence, without a major shift in policy, the world of the twenty-first century will be one of economic apartheid. There will be two dozen richer nations, a dozen or so poorer nations that have begun to close the gap with the rich, and approximately 140 poor nations slipping further behind.

Globalization of North and South

What about the U.S. administration's assumption that policies promoting U.S. business are good for overseas as well as domestic markets—that free markets and globalization raise standards of living across the board in both North and South? Here, too, the Clinton administration has missed a fundamental new reality of the global economy. As U.S. firms have shifted from local to national and now to global markets over the past half-century, a new division of winners and losers has emerged in all countries. A 1994 book, *Global Dreams: Imperial Corporations and the New World Order,* written by one of the authors and Institute for Policy Studies co-founder Richard Barnet, chronicles how powerful U.S. firms and their counterparts from England, France, Germany, and Japan are integrating only about one-third of humanity (most of those in the rich countries plus the elite of poor countries) into complex chains of production, shopping, culture, and finance.[17]

While there are enclaves in every country that are linked to these global economic webs, others are left out. Wal-Mart is spreading its superstores throughout the Western Hemisphere; millions in Latin America, though, are too poor to enjoy anything but glimpses of luxury. Citibank customers can access automated-teller machines throughout the world; the vast majority of people nevertheless borrow from the loan shark down the road. Ford Motor Company pieces together its new "global car" in Kansas City from parts made all over the globe, while executives in Detroit worry about who will be able to afford it.

Thus, while on one level the North-South gap is becoming more pronounced for the vast majority of Third World countries, on another level these global chains blur distinctions between geographical North and South. These processes create another North-South divide between the roughly one-third of humanity who comprise a "global North" of beneficiaries in every country and the two-thirds of humanity in the "global South," from the slums of New York to the favelas of Rio, who are not hooked into the new global menu of producing, consuming, and borrowing opportunities.

In contrast with the Pollyanna-ish assumptions of the Clinton administration, economic globalization, accelerated by the administration's new free-trade and investment agreements, has deepened three intractable problems that now plague almost every nation on earth, including the United States: income inequalities, job losses, and environmental damage.

Income Inequalities

The major adverse consequence of quickening global economic integration has been widening income disparity within almost all nations as the wealthier strata cash in on the opportunities of globalization, while millions of other citizens are hurt, marginalized, or left behind. Years ago, economist Simon Kuznets hypothesized that as economies develop there is initially a growth-equity trade-off, that is, income inequalities rise as nations enter the early stages of economic growth and fall in more mature economies (the so-called Kuznets curve). In the mid-1990s, however, the inequalities are growing everywhere—to such an extent that in late 1994 *The Economist* acknowledged that "it is no coincidence that the biggest increases in income inequalities have occurred in economies ... where free-market economic policies have been pursued most zealously" and that "it is a combination of lightly regulated labour markets and global economic forces that has done much more ... to favour the rich over the poor."[18]

One sees this in the perverse widening of the gap between rich and poor within nations and across the globe. Thirty years ago, the income of the richest fifth of the world's population combined was thirty times greater than that of the poorest fifth. In the mid-1990s, the income gap is more than sixty times greater.[19]

The number of billionaires grew dramatically over the past seven years, coinciding with the spread of neoliberal policies around the world. Between 1987 and 1994, the number more than doubled from 145 to 358. According to our calculations, those 358 billionaires are collectively worth some $762 billion, which is about the combined income of the world's poorest 2.5 billion people.[20] (By 2007, the world's 946 billionaires were worth a collective $3.5 trillion, the rough equivalent of the wealth of the poorest two-thirds of humanity.)[21]

Job Losses

With the exception of a few East Asian economies, every nation—North and South—is grappling with high or rising unemployment, and many, including the United States, are suffering from deteriorating working conditions for a sizable share of the workforce. Worldwide, more than 800 million people are unemployed or seriously underemployed, with tens of millions more falling into this situation each year.[22] Technology has combined with economic globalization in a devastating manner to spawn this crisis of work. Unlike previous industrial revolutions, the two most important technological innovations in recent decades—information/computers and biotechnology—destroy more jobs than they create. At the same time, rapid strides in transportation and communications technologies allow increasing numbers of jobs to be sent to countries other than the United States. Whereas a generation ago, firms shifted only apparel and consumer electronics jobs overseas, today they can move virtually the entire range of manufacturing and agricultural tasks—and a number of service jobs as well—to China, Mexico, or a range of other countries.

As many as one-third of U.S workers are swimming in a global labor pool; their jobs can be moved elsewhere, and this fact confers on their global corporate employers enhanced power to bargain down wages and working conditions. U.S. car companies, for example, can attain roughly equivalent levels of productivity and quality at their Mexican plants today as in their U.S. plants. The denial of basic worker rights in Mexico, however, severely hampers Mexican workers' efforts to negotiate improvements in their working conditions, and their wages remain a fraction of those of U.S. autoworkers. Even in Bangladesh, shirt makers are about 60 percent as productive as their American counterparts but earn only 3 to 5 percent of a U.S. salary. Hence, in many sectors, the credible threat of moving more production to Mexico and elsewhere gives the U.S. companies bargaining chips against their U.S. workers when wages and benefits are set.

In the South, roughly 38 million people enter stagnating job markets each year. As in the United States, real wages have fallen in most of Latin America and parts of Asia since the early 1980s—a shock that hits women particularly hard since they earn 30 to 40 percent less than men doing the same jobs.[23]

As job pressures grow across the South, many people leave for Europe and North America, where job markets are also tight. Violent acts of xenophobia and racism in the North are some of the ugliest manifestations of this current era of inequality and joblessness.

Environmental Damage

Just as jobs and working conditions become bargaining chips for firms in a deregulated global economy, so too do environmental standards. If the Mexican government can attract foreign firms by ignoring violations of environmental laws, it will do so, and, arguably, it must do so or lose investment. The same logic fuels the Republican Party's crusade to eliminate a wide range of environmental and other regulations in the United States.

Another pressure on the environment in the South is the constant admonition by the World Bank and the IMF to increase exports. Since most of the world's minerals, timber, fish, and land are in the South, exports tend to be natural-resource intensive. The depletion of these resources hurts yields for millions of small farmers and fishers. The frenzy to ship more goods overseas accelerates environmental degradation and thus diminishes the real, long-term wealth of Southern nations.

On the other hand, as Southern governments have rightly pointed out, most of the world's consumption, greenhouse gas emissions, ozone-depleting chemical emissions, and industrial pollution occur in the North. The heaviest burden for global environmental action rests there. But the creation of a "global North" in the South through the big-emerging-markets strategy also spreads environmental havoc. Following annual economic growth rates averaging 10 percent since 1978, China's commercial sector consumes more than one billion tons of coal annually; thus China produces nearly 11 percent of the world's carbon dioxide emissions. If this rate of climb continues, the impact on global warming will be catastrophic. In India, increased consumption will exacerbate a situation where scale already exceeds carrying capacity: Sixteen percent of the world's population is degrading just 2.3 percent of the world's land resources and 1.7 percent of its forest stock. And to compensate for falling oil revenues, Indonesia is tearing down the world's second-largest tropical rainforest, becoming the world's largest exporter of processed wood products.

Comparative Disadvantage

The North-South reality of the mid-1990s hardly matches the soothing scenario suggested by the Clinton administration. Rather, we find the ominous combination of a growing gap between the majority of the Southern and Northern countries as well as the existence of a privileged minority in a "global North" and a marginalized majority in a "global South." Indeed, our analysis suggests three sets of problems that demand attention:

- Most of the "global South"—some 45 percent of humanity who reside mainly in the 140 poorest countries of the Third World—is locked in poverty and left behind as the richer strata grow.
- Roughly 20 percent of the world's population—who are at the upper end of the two-thirds in the "global South," mainly in the big emerging markets—is beginning to enter the global consuming class in a fashion that threatens the environment and exacerbates social tensions.
- An increasing number of workers among the top one-third, or "global North," of the world is experiencing falling incomes and an erosion of worker rights and standards.

Thus far, U.S. policy has largely ignored the bottom 45 percent, concentrated on the middle 20 percent in the big emerging markets, and exacerbated the tensions within the top third. The challenge for U.S. policymakers is to focus on this new global picture with a two-tiered set of policies—one aimed at the forsaken 45 percent primarily in Southern countries and the other focused on the growing inequalities and the job and environmental crises mainly in the big emerging markets and the richer countries of the North.

The Bottom 45 Percent

The main U.S. policy arena addressing the problems of the world's poor is the debate over aid. The obsession in Washington with restructuring aid agencies will be misplaced if it does not focus on the quality of aid. As detailed in Chapter 4, any restructuring must learn from a growing number of aid experiments throughout the world that channel small amounts of funds directly to entities run by local citizen groups with guidelines that stress sustainability, participation, and equity.

While it would be a good step to redirect more aid in this manner, a great deal more needs to be done outside the realm of aid to stop the hemorrhage of resource flows from the bottom 140 countries to the North. The most fruitful avenue is to try to close the gap by taking less money out of the South rather than by getting more money in. Here the focus needs to shift back to debt. The place to begin is with the roughly 17 percent of Third World debt owed to the World Bank and the IMF—with far higher percentages owed by the poorest African nations. The World Bank and the IMF could readily use their reserves ($17 billion and $40 billion, respectively)[24] to cancel much of the outstanding debt owed to them by the poorest countries.

As governments debate World Bank restructuring, it is important to note that there are alternatives to the World Bank's formula of excessive dependence on exports and capital inflows. If the goal is to prevent nations from falling into debt again, then debt reduction can be conditioned on policies that encourage productive investment, provide assistance to small entrepreneurs and farmers, and encourage less indebted economies.

The World Bank and the Agency for International Development should also nurture the small but growing movement that is stimulating trade in goods produced under conditions that respect worker rights and the environment and recognize the deep discrimination that frequently exists against female producers. "Fair trade" entrepreneurs, with retail markets particularly strong in Europe and spreading in North America, are now responsible for hundreds of millions of dollars of trade in coffee, textiles, and other products and are developing new notions of what constitutes socially and environmentally responsible trade.

Not surprisingly, the agenda suggested for the bottom 45 percent draws from a more traditional set of remedies on how to shrink the North-South gap. However, attacking the trio of problems outlined for the global North and South—the inequities, joblessness, and environmental degradation—demands that these be implemented in conjunction with a newer set of policy instruments.

The Big Emerging Markets and Anxiety at the Top

Rather than quickening the pace to compete in an increasingly deregulated global economy, the United States can lead in calling for new rules to temper economic integration's socially and environmentally destructive effect upon unequal nations. It is important to recall that the United States rose to this same challenge on a national level in the 1930s when large firms were integrating the U.S. national economy and, in the process, playing rich unionized states off poor nonunion states. A strong trade-union movement created the momentum for Franklin Roosevelt's administration to set new national rules for minimum wages, maximum hours of work, and decent health and safety standards.

In the 1990s, this same dynamic now occurs on a global stage, where global corporations play workers and environmental standards against one another to bargain richer countries down to the standards of the poorer ones. As we have said, free-trade agreements that accelerate integration without explicitly safeguarding labor and environmental rights and standards are only deepening global job and environmental crises. Therefore, internationally recognized standards on worker rights (including freedom of association, the right to collective bargaining, and a ban on discrimination based on gender or race) and the environment, which have been hammered out by member governments of the International Labor Organization (ILO) and various international environmental treaties, need to be grafted onto new trade agreements so that firms benefiting from lower tariffs would be obligated to respect those rights and standards.

The first steps in this direction have already been taken. Since 1984, U.S. trade law has conditioned the granting of "trade preferences" to a developing country's respect for internationally recognized worker rights. Responding to popular outrage and building on this U.S. trade law,

NAFTA's negotiators crafted side-agreements that threaten minor sanctions to encourage national governments to enforce their national labor rights and environmental standards. But to be more effective, these need not only to have more teeth but also to be incorporated into the NAFTA treaty itself, as protections for corporate intellectual property now are.

In addition to social clauses on trade agreements, global corporations should be held to codes of conduct that require compliance with these rights and standards. A number of U.S. firms, including Levi Strauss and Sears, have taken a step toward comprehensive corporate codes by agreeing to voluntary codes for the firms with which they subcontract in the Third World.

New and better corporate codes and socially responsible trade and investment agreements—where key rights are truly enforced—would not solve all the world's job, environmental, and inequality problems, but they could be implemented in the short-term and would help reverse the negative dynamic we now face.

Even with the best codes of conduct and social clauses on trade agreements, increased trade is likely to continue to be based on the unsustainable exploitation of natural resources. This creates two challenges: first, to raise standards of living in the big emerging markets and other Southern nations without exceeding the earth's environmental limits and, second, to get Northern societies to acknowledge the costs to the environment of their already high standards of living. Across the board, nations—and individuals—need to acknowledge the environmental costs of economic decisions.

One way to reduce trade in natural resources (such as virgin timber) and the use of resource-intensive products (such as cars) is for governments to adopt accounting systems that factor in the real costs of natural-resource depletion and environmental degradation. In fact, technical work on "environmental accounting" is already quite advanced, as seen in the World Resources Institute's work in Costa Rica, Indonesia, and other developing countries. Even the U.S. Commerce Department has begun recalculations for a "green GDP." In this regard, the World Bank and the IMF should be required to adopt a system of "shadow pricing" that accounts for environmental costs in their projects and programs. This would be an important step in the direction of seeing "green GDPs" become the conceptual framework across the globe.

Enlightened Self-Interest

There is an impetus for a shift in policy regarding the poorer majority of the world. In the tough debate over NAFTA, citizens' groups—trade unions, environmental groups, organizations of small farmers, consumer activists, religious groups, women's groups, and others—emerged in Canada, Mexico, and the United States to press for safeguards on labor, the environment, and agriculture. While only small gains were realized in the final treaty and its labor and environment side-agreements, the democratization of the debate over international economic policy continued during the deliberations that led to the creation of the WTO in 1995, and is likely to characterize the next debates over integration in the Americas and Asia. Similar citizen coalitions throughout the world have likewise gathered momentum for reform of the World Bank and the IMF.

In other words, segments of civil society seem ahead of U.S. policy-makers in comprehending that the widening inequalities within nations and between North and South pose crucial challenges that are in our enlightened self-interest to meet. Working conditions in a number of Third World countries have an increasing impact on working conditions in the United States. Growing inequalities in the South are increasing the flow of people, drugs, and environmental problems into the North. The rapid rise of the rich and the emergence of a middle class in the big emerging markets increase instability and tension vis-a-vis the vast numbers of people left behind—witness the growing labor unrest in China, Indonesia, and Mexico, as well as the continuing rebellion in Mexico's Chiapas state.

While the Clinton administration can continue to respond belatedly to crises and fall back on its faulty assumptions about the North-South economic reality, the attendant problems of the post–Cold War global economy will inevitably become clearer as an increasing number of people in the North and South are hurt. There is no way to get around the need for a fundamental rethinking of the North-South agenda. The question is simply whether the United States will take the lead in resolving these problems or will instead wait and be led.

Chapter 6

The Washington Consensus Cracks

The chapter that follows marks our final stop in the twentieth century. We pause at a point almost two decades into the Washington Consensus. It is a watershed moment just months before what became arguably the most public confrontation between Washington Consensus backers and opponents: the November 1999 meeting of the World Trade Organization in Seattle, Washington. By then, the more country-specific and fledgling citizen opposition we observed in our earlier time travel had transformed into a strong, organized, global, and multisectoral citizen opposition to Consensus policies and institutions—the alter-globalization movement.

Also significant, as you are about to observe in the current chapter, a number of prominent elite players began publicly to distance themselves from parts of the Consensus. Indeed, we touch ground just after the key historical event that catalyzed this dissent: the 1997–1998 global financial crisis, often referred to as the East Asian crisis. That crisis was widely seen as the result of Southern governments having given in to Consensus dictates to remove safeguards on their financial markets. Thus, the crisis was viewed as a refutation of at least one tenet of the Consensus that had previously been gaining momentum. But, to say that the 1997–1998 financial crisis shook elite circles is an understatement. The "revolutionary" free-market fundamentalist dictum that governments had little or no role to play in development could no longer be defended. And the single-minded Consensus focus on economic growth also came in for questioning in certain elite circles.

In the period from 1997 until our chapter opens in 1999, there were clear indications that the balance of power had begun to shift. As you are about to witness, victories that had once seemed unimaginable were achieved by the alter-globalization movement. One case in point (we will leave more details for the chapter) occurred in 1998, when global citizen groups showed their growing sophistication and power in a victorious campaign to force Northern governments to abandon proposals (the so-called Multilateral Agreement on Investment) that would strengthen protections for global corporations.

Seattle then proved to be a convergence for the opposition, and it became the stage where twenty years of pent-up citizen anger and frustration with market fundamentalism boiled over onto the streets to confront Consensus backers. The mainstream media focused on small groups of protesters blockading the streets or breaking windows; largely off camera, however, teach-ins, vigils, public debates, and mass marches animated Seattle for a full week. Another key development also occurred largely off camera as the city was shut down: Organized civil society "in the streets" was finding common cause with some representatives of poorer country governments "in the suites" who were publicly breaking away from parts of the Consensus. Together, these two groupings forced the trade meetings to shut down in failure.

The events of the mid- to late 1990s created cracks in the Consensus that could not be mended. Humpty Dumpty had fallen—and, as will be seen in later chapters, was not to be put back together again.

The times they were palpably a-changing.

$$\text{⊰——⊱}$$

1999—As we have seen in our journey thus far, between the early 1980s and the late 1990s, an elite consensus swept the globe that unfettered free markets provided the formula to make rich countries out of poor.

At the turn of the century, however, deep cracks have appeared within this so-called Washington Consensus. Its legitimacy has come into question in the face of an increasingly effective citizens' backlash in North and South, and there is growing dissension within the ranks of Consensus backers, as the effects of the financial crisis of the late 1990s are felt around the globe. While not yet dead, the Consensus has been wounded—and potentially fatally so.

This chapter analyzes the reign of the Washington Consensus and what we see as its loss of legitimacy in the global economic upheavals of recent years. It is written neither to help rebuild the Consensus nor to mourn its possible fall. Let us be clear from the start: We were never part of the

Consensus. In what we have written since the early years of the Consensus, we have chronicled the human and environmental wreckage of Consensus policies. Previous chapters dissect the reign; our goal here is to analyze the cracks in the Consensus, and to reflect upon the lessons learned in terms of a new development agenda.

What is needed, we argue, is not a new Washington-driven and Washington-dominated consensus, but a vibrant new debate, a debate that must involve the supposed beneficiaries of development—workers, farmers, the urban poor, indigenous communities, and so on—in determining the goals and policies of new paths to development.

The power of the Washington Consensus over development theory and practice in the 1980s and 1990s is hard to overstate. That once vibrant debate about development all but disappeared as the Consensus took on almost religious qualities. The high priests of the Consensus—the U.S. Department of Treasury, the International Monetary Fund (IMF), and the World Bank—were in Washington. Converts to the cult of the Consensus spread far beyond the Beltway—as with other religions, through a combination of the appeal of its simplicity, proselytizing by its believers, and outright coercion.

Attacking the Consensus

Yet, even as the steamroller plowed on, the Consensus never gained widespread legitimacy in the developing world outside of a technocratic elite and parts of the small middle class. As the 1980s unfolded, citizen groups in the South, often campaigning in collaboration with Northern environmental, labor, and antipoverty groups, exposed the adverse development impact of the policies of the World Bank and the IMF, the two institutions that have most zealously enforced the Washington Consensus. From the Philippines to Mexico to Ghana came evidence that the free-market policies of the Consensus were having negative effects on workers, the environment, and equity.

As we have seen, citizen outcry against the neoliberal policies of the Washington Consensus was not limited to the South. Environmentalists in the North began launching campaigns against the damaging environmental impact of the World Bank policies in the early 1980s. Labor unions in developed countries jumped on the anti-free-market bandwagon as companies used the threat of moving production to China or Mexico to bargain down wages and benefits.[1]

As free-trade policies implemented in the South rebounded with adverse effects on factory workers, small farmers, and small businesses in the North, public opinion polls in the United States began to show that a majority of Americans were skeptical of the merits of free trade. By the end of 1998, the U.S. public was not simply opposed to expansion of the free-trade agenda: According to a December 1998 *Wall Street Journal*/NBC News survey, 58 percent of Americans polled said that "foreign trade has been bad for the U.S. economy."[2]

The broad public opposition in the North gained backing in diverse elite circles during the battles over free trade in the 1990s. In the United States, many Democratic members of Congress began to call for "fair trade"—a critique that in many ways mirrored the cry in organized civil society in the South. On the other side of the aisle, roughly sixty to seventy Republican members of Congress have consistently opposed free-trade agreements. While the Republican and the "fair trade" camps opposed to free trade diverge dramatically on an alternative vision, the two camps have, on key occasions, joined forces to slow the advance of market fundamentalism.

Indeed, by the late 1990s, anti-free-trade forces were strong enough to stall new free-trade and investment initiatives from the U.S. government; notably, legislation granting "fast track" trade authority to the president went down in defeat in 1997 and 1998. An even more significant victory came on a global level with the derailing of the Multilateral Agreement on Investment (MAI). The MAI was an initiative to expand the reach of the Washington Consensus by requiring governments (read Southern governments) to treat global corporations the same as local business. But a combination of very sophisticated work on the part of organized civil society (especially in East Asia, Europe, and Canada) and elite misgivings following the Asian financial crisis (described below) led to its collapse.[3]

If the combined strength of these outside critics slowed the momentum of the Washington Consensus, it was the 1997 Asian financial crisis that shook its very foundations.

In order to understand the actual cracks that have appeared within the Consensus, it is necessary to understand the roots of the financial crisis.

Hot Money

During the 1990s, the World Bank, the IMF, and the U.S. Treasury expanded their initial focus from the free-trade and longer-term investment strand of the Consensus to the financial planks, "encouraging" governments around the globe to open their stock markets and financial markets to short-term investments from the North. The resulting quick injections of capital from mutual funds, pension funds, and other sources propelled short-term growth in the 1990s, but also encouraged bad lending and bad investing.

Between 1990 and 1996, the amount of annual private financial flows entering poorer nations skyrocketed from $44 billion to $244 billion. Roughly half of this was long-term direct investment, but most of the rest—as recipient countries were soon to discover—was footloose, moving from country to country at the tap of a computer keyboard.

In mid-1997, as the reality of this shortsighted lending and investing began to surface, first in Thailand, then in South Korea, and then in several other countries, Northern investors and speculators panicked. Their "hot money" fled much faster than it had arrived—leaving local economies without the capital they had come to depend on. Currency speculators exacerbated the crisis by betting against the local currencies of the crisis nations, sending local currency values to new lows.

IMF advice seemed only to quicken the exodus of capital. Currencies and stock markets from South Korea to Brazil nose-dived. And, as these nations slashed purchases of everything from oil to wheat, prices of these products likewise plummeted. The financial crisis stalled production and trade in such large economies as Indonesia, Russia, South Korea, and Brazil, leaving in its wake widespread pain, dislocation, and environmental ruin. Exact figures are hard to come by, but the main international trade union federation estimates that, by the end of 1999, some twenty-seven million workers in the five worst hit Asian countries—Indonesia, South Korea, Thailand, Malaysia, and the Philippines—will have lost their jobs.[4]

As economies collapsed, elite support for the Washington Consensus began to crumble. In the pages of the *Wall Street Journal,* former U.S. secretary of defense Robert McNamara likened the crisis to the Vietnam War, implying that then U.S. Treasury secretary Robert Rubin, his deputy and successor Larry Summers, IMF managing director Michel Camdessus, and the other top managers had lost control.

Elite Dissent

Two sets of elite actors began launching critiques at Rubin, Summers, and Camdessus—not quietly, but in a very public and vocal fashion, using the op-ed pages of the *New York Times,* the *Wall Street Journal,* and the *Washington Post* to make their cases. One group, led by such prominent free-trade economists as Jagdish Bhagwati of Columbia University, Paul Krugman of MIT, and World Bank chief economist Joseph Stiglitz, supports free markets for trade but not for short-term capital. (The group also includes such well-known Washington figures as Henry Kissinger.) Bhagwati argues that capital markets are by their nature unstable and require controls. Krugman outlines the case for exchange controls as a response to crisis.

However, as dramatically interventionist as some of their proposals are and as heated as the debate may sound, these critics largely seek to repair the cracks in the Consensus—by allowing national exchange and/or capital controls under certain circumstances—not to tear down the entire neoliberal edifice.

Some within this first set of Consensus reformers have focused more on the folly of IMF policies during the crisis. Some prominent economists, such as Harvard's Jeffrey Sachs, himself once a proponent of "shock therapy" in Russia, faulted the IMF for prescribing recessionary policies that transformed a liquidity crisis into a full-fledged financial panic and subsequently into a collapse of the real economy in an expanding list of countries. "Instead of dousing the fire," Sachs wrote in 1998, "the IMF in effect screamed fire in the theater."[5] While still subscribing to the goal of free trade, Sachs and others argue that the IMF needs to revise its standard formula for economic reform, make its decision making more transparent, and become more publicly accountable for the impact of its policies.

A second set of Consensus dissidents—which we term the "ultra free-market camp"—goes further in criticizing the IMF, arguing for its abolition. The critique of this group is rooted in an extreme defense of free markets, and its members fault the IMF for interfering in the markets. They charge that IMF monies disbursed to debtor governments end up being used to bail out investors, thus eliminating the discipline of risk (or "moral hazard") in private markets. This group is led by such longtime free-trade supporters as the Heritage Foundation and the Cato Institute (whose opposition to publicly funded aid institutions is nothing new), but its ranks have swelled with such well-known, vocal converts as former Citicorp CEO Walter Wriston, former U.S. secretary of state George Shultz, and former U.S. secretary of the treasury William E. Simon.[6]

These two camps of elite dissent within the Consensus in the United States have their counterparts in other rich nations and among some developing country governments. West European economies, while not in the dire straits of Japan and much of the rest of the world, continue to be plagued by high unemployment, and their new joint currency, the Euro, has gotten off to a shaky start. The European Union has also been involved in widely publicized trade disputes with the United States, several involving the European public's growing skepticism over genetically engineered foods.

As a result, a number of politicians in center-left governments in Europe have raised their voices to question parts of the Consensus. Even the U.S.

administration's closest ally, British prime minister Tony Blair, has a reform plan that includes a new intergovernmental global financial authority to help prevent future financial crises. Most Western European governments support at least limited capital controls. And some members of the Canadian parliament are supporting an international tax on foreign currency transactions to discourage speculative transactions.

Japan is also looking for openings to rewrite parts of the Consensus. The Japanese government has been both weakened and disillusioned by a decade of recession. Over the past two years, it has waged high-profile fights with the United States over Japan's proposal to create an Asian economic fund to help countries in crisis, and over whether a Thai candidate backed by Japan and much of Asia, or a New Zealander backed by most of the North, should lead the World Trade Organization (a compromise was worked out whereby each served half of the term).

In the developing world, there have also been a number of recent instances where elite actors have departed from specific aspects of Consensus policies. In Hong Kong, long heralded by Consensus adherents as a supreme example of free-market trade and finance policies, the government reacted to the crisis spreading through Asia by intervening in the stock market and acting to prevent currency speculation. Malaysia grabbed the world's attention in 1998 by imposing a series of capital and exchange controls that were successful in stemming short-term speculative flows. Several developing-country governments have moved beyond their discontent over certain IMF prescriptions to openly question whether the World Trade Organization should heed American and European calls for new global trade talks to further liberalize foreign investment rules and agricultural protections among member states.

The combination of these criticisms and actions has begun to influence even the IMF and the World Bank. In Indonesia, where the crisis has been particularly brutal, the IMF implicitly acknowledged that there were occasions when the costs of Consensus policies were likely to be unacceptably high. Initially the IMF hung tough—until riots greeted the removal of price subsidies on fuel and precipitated a chain of events that actually led to the fall of the long-reigning Indonesian dictator Suharto.[7] In its dealings with the post-Suharto government, the Fund responded positively to the pleas of the Jakarta government for increased social spending and the maintenance of subsidized prices for fuel, food, and other necessities.

Since coming on board as World Bank president in 1995, James Wolfensohn has taken small steps—at least in rhetoric—to distance himself and his institution from the more orthodox policies of the IMF. In 1997, he agreed to carry out a multicountry review of the Bank's structural adjustment policies with several hundred nongovernmental organizations (NGOs) led by the Development Group for Alternative Policies. His speeches and the Bank's publications have included acknowledgment of the social and environmental costs of Consensus policies.[8] And, he launched what was billed as a major change of policy: the Heavily Indebted Poor Countries (HIPC) initiative, which the Bank and Fund created in 1996 to offer some debt reduction to some extremely poor nations if they implemented a multiyear package of stringent structural adjustment.[9]

In the final analysis, however, these elite dissenters share a strategic goal: to salvage the overall message of neoliberalism, while modifying the pillar of free capital flows. Indeed, the heat of the debate between these elite critics and such Consensus adherents as Michel Camdessus of the IMF and Secretary of the Treasury Larry Summers over capital mobility has made it easy for observers to overlook a key reality: The Consensus still largely holds with respect to trade policy.

Cracks in the Consensus

Even though it is not the goal of the elite dissenters to kill neoliberalism, the appearance of any dissent at all is significant. Dissent from within ranks had been unheard of in the last two decades during which the Consensus advanced seemingly unchecked. Now, in their tinkering with the ten commandments of the Consensus and in their desire to capture the limelight, elite critics are not only undermining the legitimacy and credibility of the Consensus but are also unwittingly opening the door to broader mass-based, anti-free-market criticism. These elite critiques have opened cracks in the Consensus in three key areas, cracks that could become deadly fissures at the hands of outside critics.

First, there is the question of in whose interests Consensus policies are sculpted. The language some use in their elite critiques raises questions about the narrow interests that the Consensus serves. Free-trade champion Jagdish Bhagwati, writing in *Foreign Affairs,* has decried liberalized capital mobility across borders as the work of the "Wall Street–Treasury complex" (a term that builds on President Eisenhower's warnings of a "military-industrial complex").[10] Bhagwati points fingers at individuals who have moved between Wall Street financial firms and the highest echelons of the U.S. government and who, in Bhagwati's surprisingly stinging words, are "unable to look much beyond the interest of Wall Street, which it equates with the good of the world."[11] This should create ammunition for the outsider critique: If the U.S. Treasury (and international financial institutions) are not able to look beyond such narrow "special interests" in terms of capital, why should they be trusted to do so with broader economic policies?

Second, what goals should economic policies serve and who should deter-mine these goals? One of the elite critics, the World Bank's Joseph Stiglitz, has begun to call for a "post-Washington Consensus" that moves beyond the narrow goal of economic growth to the more expansive goal of sustainable, equitable, and democratic development.[12] In speeches that have surprised many observers, Stiglitz argues that the debate over national economic policies and the debate over the new global economy must be democratized. For example, he says, workers must be invited to sit at the table when their country's eco-nomic policies are being discussed in order to be able to argue against policies that hurt them. Outside critics need to push for Stiglitz's words to be turned into action. Why not invite workers—and environmentalists and farmers and others—who represent the broader national interests to participate now?[13]

Third, the elite dissenters are reigniting the Keynesian belief that the state has a legitimate role in development. Indeed, whatever comes of the global financial crisis, the widespread fear of an unregulated global casino that can devastate individual economies overnight is negating the Con-sensus rejection of an activist state role. While most elite critics will now concede the need for a government role in the realm of short-term financial flows, outside critics of neoliberalism should exploit this crack to open up a larger debate about government intervention. With the acknowledgment that government is needed to check the markets on one front, there can be more intelligent debate over the role of government in other areas. The development debate, so lively in the 1960s and 1970s and so stifled in the 1980s and 1990s, can be revived.

High Priests Respond

In the face of the spreading dissent and criticism, the U.S. Treasury Depart-ment is attempting to hold the line. Triumphant, with its booming stock market, its low unemployment and inflation, and its victory in Kosovo, the U.S. government is trying to reassert a Wall Street–centered approach that differs from the old one only in minor details. Mild U.S. Treasury propos-als to increase statistical disclosure by financial institutions and improve surveillance of national economic policies by the IMF won the day at the 1999 meeting of the Group of Eight in Cologne, Germany. Secretary of the Treasury Larry Summers and his minions will attempt to consolidate their agenda and glue some of the cracks together at the final IMF and World Bank annual meeting of the twentieth century.

Among most leading Consensus pundits outside of the ranks of the IMF and the U.S. Treasury Department, however, there is a new—admittedly begrudging—acknowledgement that the Consensus has lost much of its legitimacy in the view of the public and that there is a need to factor more social and environmental concerns into economic policies. In this climate of elite discord, there is greater space for the citizen groups on the outside to press for more far-reaching and desperately needed reforms in global economic institutions.

At key moments in the recent past, unions, environmentalists, and other citizen groups have grown strong enough to stall the implementation of Consensus policies, as we have seen in the fights over fast-track authority and the Multilateral Agreement on Investment in the late 1990s.

The challenge now for these outsiders is to exploit the internal discord among Consensus supporters, to establish links with dissident voices within governments, and to fire up the debate over development goals and the role of government. The Philippine social scientist Walden Bello sums up the clamor of citizens for change around the world with this sentence: "It's the development model, stupid."

A New Development Debate

New development proposals from citizen groups are based on both expansive goals and trade and finance policies that would shift the beneficiaries of these policies from a narrow group of corporations and wealthy individuals to a much broader swath of the public.

On the trade front, the upcoming ministerial meeting of the WTO, to be hosted by President Clinton in Seattle in November 1999, will provide a dramatic backdrop to a major confrontation over the future of trade rules. Joining several developing-country governments in opposing an expansion of trade and investment liberalization will be tens of thousands of organized steelworkers and apparel workers, family farmers, members of Ralph Nader's Public Citizen, and environmentalists who are planning a week of educational activities and protests.

Labor unions are calling for a halt in new talks on all issues except strengthening workers' protections under WTO rules. Other citizen groups want to prune back the WTO's powers in favor of once again permitting individual governments to set investment and government procurement rules and to declare food safety and environmental rules off limits to challenges by other nations—that is, keeping open the remaining "development space" that governments still have.[14]

On the finance front, future IMF and World Bank annual meetings should provide a venue for bringing into focus the different agendas for a "new financial architecture" as well as the issue of debt relief for poor nations. Many of the same citizen groups that led the trade fight have shifted their attention to addressing the financial crisis. For example, Friends of the Earth, the International Forum on Globalization, the AFL-CIO, the Malaysia–based Third World Network, and Thailand–based Focus on the Global South have convened hundreds of experts—activists and researchers—from both North and South to sketch out an institutional framework that would reorient financial flows from speculation to long-term investment at the local and national levels.[15]

Collectively, these proposals suggest that local and national governments should be given greater authority to use the so-called development space to set exchange rate policies, regulate capital flows, and eliminate speculative activity. A priority at the international level is the creation of an international bankruptcy mechanism outside the IMF. When a country cannot repay its debts, the mechanism would oversee a debt restructuring in which there would be a public and private sharing of costs. When the next Indonesia, Russia, or Brazil teeters on the brink of a deep financial crisis, it would turn to this mechanism, not to the IMF, for help. With such a facility in place, the IMF could return to its more modest original mandate as lender of last resort as well as sponsor of a venue for the open exchange of financial and economic information or, better yet, another non-Washington-based institution could take over these roles.

Alter-globalization groups, led by religious coalitions in many countries and rallying under the banner of Jubilee 2000, have critiqued the HIPC debt-relief initiative as too paltry, as too connected to the same old onerous neoliberal conditions, and as bypassing too many debt-burdened countries. They argue that current debt-reduction initiatives should be transformed to cancel more significant amounts of debt, and that debt reduction should not be conditioned on a country's adherence to IMF and World Bank austerity policies.

Finally, many critics are picking up on an old proposal by Nobel Prize–winner James Tobin of Yale University, who suggested a tiny global tax on foreign currency transactions. In today's flourishing global financial casino, such a currency transaction tax (often termed a "Tobin tax") would both discourage harmful speculation and generate revenues that could help the nations in crisis.

The growing strength of citizen opposition, however, has not yet been translated into a new overall consensus based on such proposals. Much as we would like to be town criers heralding the death of market fundamentalism, such news is premature at the turn of the century. Too many members of the policymaking elite, particularly in the United States, still cling to the precepts of the old consensus, especially vis-à-vis trade. While another global economic downturn would no doubt lend weight to the outsider critique, the future of these opposition proposals depends in the final analysis on the political sophistication of their proponents. Can citizen movements translate growing discontent into effective political pressure both at a national level and jointly in the WTO, the IMF, and the World Bank? Can they shift the debate beyond the confines of the free-market dogma of the Washington Consensus?

In the closing months of the Second World War, a small group made up primarily of men from the richer countries sketched the architecture of the postwar global economy. The institutions they created are no longer serving the needs of the majority of people on earth. As we approach the new century, there is at last the opportunity for a larger, more representative group to create new global rules and institutions for the twenty-first century.

Chapter 7

Post-9/11: Myths About Aid and Trade Resurface

In our final travel back in time, we revisit the Washington Consensus over halfway through the first decade of the twenty-first century, to capture the rapidly changing world of post–September 11. Our previous time travel, at the turn of the century, revealed significant cracks in the elite backing of the Consensus. A full-fledged debate on several key Consensus points had emerged, and we hoped that the years that followed would find growing elite admission of the bankruptcy of neoliberalism writ large—and a return to the key questions of "What is development?" and "Development for whom?"

But historical trajectories seldom follow straight lines. The historical moment and momentum shifted. As you are about to see when we touch ground in 2006, the Consensus was given new life with the terrorist attacks of September 11, 2001. The U.S. administration of George W. Bush brazenly asserted that free-market policies were the best solution to the global poverty that bred terrorism. This argument was used by the United States to launch a new round of WTO negotiations (alternatively called the Doha Round, or the Development Round) in 2001 to try to further strengthen trade and financial liberalization while weakening individual government control over economic decisions.

Yet, as we have just witnessed in our time travels, Humpty Dumpty had already cracked. This created a fascinating, but dangerous, give and take between Consensus backers and opponents. Into this volatile mix jumped two prominent U.S. intellectuals to confuse the debate further: The *New York Times*'s Thomas Friedman and Columbia University's Jeffrey Sachs have been typecast as enlightened elite dissenters to the Consensus. Each amassed followers among elite "break-aways" as well as among civil-society groups. Each wrote highly influential books in the opening years of the new century, Friedman's *The World Is Flat* and Sachs's *The End of Poverty.* Untangling the confusion they spread as they, in fact, reinforced key Consensus pillars is the subject of this chapter.

We argue that Sachs and Friedman have dusted off old Consensus myths about stimulating economic growth through more aid and "freer" trade—but have wrapped them in an eye-catching (but faulty) new package of ending poverty. As we did with the Washington Consensus in our prior travel, we put their analyses under a "development" microscope. Our analytical frame remains the same: What is development? And, development for whom?

The moment we have chosen for our time travel is an important one in the conflict between Consensus backers and the alter-globalization movement. In the half-decade after September 11, mass protests by the alter-globalization movement were fewer and smaller. Some observers, especially in the U.S. media, focused on the smaller size of demonstrations in the North to declare the "anti-globalization" movement dead. What we two see, however, is the evolution of a dynamic movement—an evolution away from the age of mass protest that had its denouement in Seattle in 1999.

Rather, in the dawning years of the twenty-first century, the alter-movements entered a new era. This new era was marked, in part, by mass citizen gatherings to propose alternatives to neoliberalism. Some occurred under the rubric of the World Social Forum's annual (or biannual) global meetings, often with more than 100,000 participants, as well as a series of related regional and national gatherings (including a U.S. Social Forum in 2007). In addition, around the world, at the local, national, regional, and global levels, alternatives to the old Consensus were being launched on the ground. And, in more than a half-dozen Latin American countries, popular discontent with neoliberalism helped elect governments challenging at least parts of the Consensus.

The stage was set for an intensification of the development debate. Enter Jeff Sachs and Thomas Friedman and their attempts to salvage the Consensus through "more aid and trade." Hang on tight as we travel to 2006.

⊶——⊷

2006—Thomas Friedman and Jeffrey Sachs—articulate, learned globetrotting pundits—would seem an unlikely duo to hijack the development debate.

Yet, through their best-selling books—Friedman's *The World Is Flat* and Sachs's *The End of Poverty*—their prominent exposure in the U.S. media, and endorsements by celebrities like Bono, the superstar lead singer of the rock group U2, they have attempted to do precisely that.[1] Just a half-decade after protests by citizen groups in Latin America and elsewhere helped discredit two decades of market-oriented neoliberal dogma, Friedman and Sachs have tried to rally support with simplistic slogans of "more aid" and "more trade." In doing so, they have put forward myths, some new and some old, about the poor, economic development, and the global economy.

In many ways, Friedman and Sachs are leading us backward to the era that began with the ascendancy of Ronald Reagan, Margaret Thatcher, and Helmut Kohl in the early 1980s. As we have seen, those free-market icons ushered in almost two decades of a one-size-fits-all approach to economic growth: privatization, government deregulation, and fewer barriers to trade and financial flows. These neoliberal market-opening policies were pressed on dozens of poor, indebted nations by the World Bank, the International Monetary Fund (IMF), and the U.S. government. Trade and foreign investment surged; though many large corporations and consumers benefited, a heavy toll was too often visited on the poor, workers, and the environment. In the late 1990s, a global backlash of citizen protest erupted as the financial crisis of 1997–1998 plunged hundreds of millions into poverty in Asia, Russia, and Brazil.

For those in the United States, this backlash was most visible in the "Battle of Seattle" in late 1999, in which massive demonstrations shut down a World Trade Organization (WTO) ministerial meeting. But this was hardly a localized phenomenon: Elsewhere, activists reacted against the growing power of global corporations, which pitted workers, communities, and nations against one another in "a race to the bottom." As corporations spread sweatshops to Mexico, China, Indonesia, and elsewhere, workers demanded that they respect such core rights as the right to organize. Environmentalists struggled to maintain hard-won protections in the face of pressure from international investors. Farmers protested against land-grabbing by corporate agribusiness. As privatization of basic services shifted wealth from government coffers into the pockets of private investors and increased the cost of water, electricity, and other basic services, citizen groups in Bolivia, Ghana, Uruguay, Argentina, and elsewhere fought off water privatization efforts and successfully replaced privatized systems with various models of public control.[2] Since the election of Hugo Chávez as president of Venezuela in 1998, the electorates in more than a half-dozen Latin American countries have rejected governments that supported neoliberalsim.

Although no new consensus emerged in the late 1990s, officials in key public and private institutions began to consider alternative approaches to the neoliberal dogma. Following the global financial crisis, the IMF accepted the need for some controls on capital flows. Amid the dislocations wrought by the building of dams and other large infrastructure projects, the World Bank claimed to be reassessing the environmental and social costs of such undertakings. A number of global corporations jumped on the social responsibility bandwagon. Experts at the United Nations Development Program and elsewhere suggested that "human development" and human-rights indexes were better gauges of success than crude and aggregated income measures.

However, the steady movement away from market fundamentalism was interrupted by the September 11 terrorist attacks on New York and Washington. The U.S. administration of George W. Bush seized the moment to argue that opening markets was an essential weapon in the "global war on terrorism." In its September 2002 National Security Strategy, the administration cited poverty as one of the root causes of the terrorist impulse. Washington once again began to push open-market policies as the best solution to the problem of endemic poverty.

This is the context into which Friedman and Sachs splashed onto best-seller lists to reinforce the administration's misguided focus. This may sound like heresy to some readers. After all, Jeffrey Sachs ventured with Bono to remote villages in Africa and brought the plight of the world's poorest to the readers of *Time* magazine.[3] He helped popularize the concept of "ending poverty" and opened space for citizen groups to launch a "global campaign against poverty" that has touched the hearts and pocketbooks of millions in dozens of countries. He also helped to put poverty on the agenda at the G-8 Summit in Edinburgh in 2005. Thomas Friedman, in his columns for the *New York Times* and other writings, has painted a picture of high-tech prosperity, a "flat earth" where every individual has an equal chance to get ahead.

Therefore, it should come as no surprise that there is a tendency to read their books and sigh with relief: There are straightforward answers to ending poverty and spreading prosperity. As Friedman reassures us: "We know the basic formula for economic success."[4] Unfortunately, their work rests on dubious "facts" about the poor, about technology and the "development ladder," about aid, about trade and open markets, and, perhaps most importantly, about the choices we face. From our own work in the Philippines and other poor nations and through discussions with members of a poverty working group of the International Forum on Globalization,[5] we believe that Friedman and Sachs, in having accepted certain myths about development, are leading us down the wrong path. Of the five myths we analyze below, the first one adds something new to the traditional Washington Consensus lens because it deals with the overall poverty frame that Sachs has constructed and that some other Consensus backers have embraced.

Myth #1: The primary focus should be on extreme poverty, as defined by per capita income of less than a dollar a day, rather than on broader quality-of-life indicators, including the empowerment of the poor.

From his perch at Columbia University's Earth Institute, Jeffrey Sachs has spent a good deal of time attempting to measure poverty. By his estimates (he borrows heavily on data from the World Bank and the United Nations), roughly a sixth of humanity (1.1 billion) are "extremely poor," eking out a bare existence on less than one dollar a day. Another 1.5 billion are "moderately poor," subsisting on one to two dollars a day. And another billion are "relatively poor," earning less than what economists suggest is necessary to meet their basic needs. Sachs challenges us to end extreme poverty by 2025; the United Nations, which he advises, seeks to halve it by 2015 as part of its Millennium Development Goals. These goals are not only morally right, says Sachs, they are achievable. We can take heart since the ranks of the extreme poor are already down from 1.5 billion in 1981 to 1.1 billion today.

The problem with these "facts" is that if you eliminate China, India, and other fast-growing Asian nations, the number of "extreme poor" has stayed fairly level during this period, and has grown steadily in Africa.[6] Another major limitation of Sachs's approach, shared by many development agencies and anti-poverty crusaders, is that it relies overwhelmingly on poverty measures that appear deceptively precise. The fact that someone lives on less than two dollars a day actually tells us very little about that person's real condition. In countries such as South Africa, where government services are generous, one dollar a day goes further than in Haiti. Furthermore, as nations grow rapidly, as have China and India over the past decade and a half, the amount of money needed for people in the cash economy to maintain a decent standard of living also rises.[7]

For many of the 1.1 billion who subsist in rural areas on less than one dollar a day (over 300 million of whom are indigenous peoples), life changed little for centuries until the last few decades. Most live in rural or fishing communities where they have some control over the natural resources on which they depend for their livelihoods. They consume much of what they produce and barter for some of the rest of what they need. They live in self-built homes and depend on traditional medicines. While their poverty may be "extreme" by Sachs's monetary measure, their quality of life is typically much better than that of their urban counterparts, even though their incomes are often smaller. While most would undoubtedly like more economic, social (e.g., health and education), and political "security," their basic needs and sense of community and purpose have, until recently, remained largely intact.

Our experience living with poor families in rural areas suggests that it has been the opening of their natural resources to global agribusiness, factory fishing fleets, and corporate interests that often leads to real poverty. Millions have been pushed off their land over the past few generations into urban slums where they live in squalor, earning pennies a day from "informal" activities like hawking cigarettes on the street or bringing home a few dollars a day from a sweatshop where they sew clothes for consumers across the ocean. Their plight is extreme: They are hungry much of the time (even before the food price crisis of 2008), they lack clean water, they cannot afford doctors, community supports are few, and hope is a sparse commodity. Thus, as farm families are pushed into urban slums, the number of people living in misery and squalor in a particular country may rise even as the monetary measures of poverty decline. In sum, the statistics upon which most poverty elimination strategies are based are extremely misleading, and often steer experts toward the wrong solutions.

Myth #2: Development is a linear process of individuals from all walks of life using new technologies to move up a modernization ladder.

Sachs suggests that we focus our energy on cleaning up pockets of extreme poverty so that the impoverished are able to get a leg up on the "ladder of development." We need to give them "a boost up to the first rung . . . so that they may begin their own ascent."[8] Friedman picks up the same theme: "Ill health also traps people in poverty," he writes, and "keeps them from grasping the first rung of the ladder."[9] Once released from the bonds of extreme poverty, "a kid in India with a cheap PC can learn the inner workings of the same operating system that is running in some of the largest data centers of corporate America."[10] State power and corporate power count for less in a "plug-and-play world."[11]

In Friedman's world, anyone who is not lazy (unlike those in Latin America where "everyone sleeps until midmorning")[12] can join the dynamic "flat world" economy by finding a laptop and jumping into the global rat race. According to Friedman, the entry of China, India, and the former Soviet Union into the global economy in the past fifteen years has added 3 billion people to this new economy. Then, quietly on page 375, Friedman confesses that "the world is not flat. . . ." "Hundreds of millions" are "left behind by the flattening." Eight pages later, he acknowledges that the high-tech flat earth economy in India provides only 0.2 percent of India's jobs.[13]

Sachs does reflect on the causes of poverty. But his poverty-creation story also is linear: Almost all people the world over were poor and living on farms a couple of centuries ago. He dismisses the notion that "the rich have gotten rich *because* the poor have gotten poor."[14] As Sachs has it, those with access to technology and trade got wealthier, while those geographically isolated or in areas prone to natural disasters and disease got left behind.

As a result, Sachs's quick fixes are technological: "We glimpse the pivotal roles that science and technology play in the development process. And we sense a progression of development that moves from subsistence agriculture toward light manufacturing and urbanization, and on to high-tech services."[15] To get a person with a middle-class "state of mind"[16] out of poverty, Friedman says, give that person access to a computer. "Guilty as charged," Friedman says in response to criticisms of himself as a "technological determinist."[17]

One major problem is that this focus on technology is ahistorical. As the Indian physicist Vandana Shiva writes: "Ending poverty requires knowing how poverty is created."[18] This sounds simple, but it gets to the crux of why so much of the development debate is misguided and so much money has been wasted in the name of ending poverty. Our experience suggests that laziness and corruption—Friedman's culprits—are not the root causes of this failure. Nor are Sachs's accidents of geography and climate.

Rather, the history of most parts of the world suggests a more violent process of poverty creation rooted in unequal power relations and manifested through slavery, the colonial legacy of export economies, the presence of extractive industries, and the sale of natural resources by governments to the highest corporate bidders.[19] For much of the past century, the U.S. government supported dictators who impoverished their people by plundering their countries' resources.

Our three decades of travel and research lead us to the conclusion that most people who are poor have been marginalized by more powerful actors, be they landlords or corporations or governments. Poverty is not simply an absolute condition; it needs to be understood as a dynamic. It is necessary to look at the social, economic, and political interactions of poor people with the elites. It is not a matter of "cleaning up" disease; even healthy people are easily pushed back into extreme poverty when the deeper structural roots of poverty are not dealt with. That "ladder of development" is actually a complex, multidimensional maze of power relations. (As you will recall, in Chapter 4 we debunked a related myth that poor people are the cause of environmental problems.)

In this context, we would argue that rising inequality is as important an indicator of human development as is poverty.[20] Earlier in this book, we have presented evidence that economic globalization has contributed to a

global economic apartheid: the widening gap between its wealthy beneficiaries and the marginalized within most nations, and the growing divide
between most poor nations (excluding China, India, Brazil, and a handful
of other big emerging markets) and the club of rich nations. We have also
argued that growing inequality within a nation falls hardest on the poor;
substantial evidence continues to support our contentions.[21] Contrary to
Sachs and Friedman, we believe that growing inequality is the inevitable
outcome of the past two decades of market-opening policies. In China,
for example, in order to create an entrepreneurial class, the government
deliberately abandoned public universal health care and education, leaving
millions to fend for themselves.

Myth #3: More and better aid is a big part of the answer.

This myth has much staying power. (We saw one permutation of this
in Chapter 4 vis-à-vis aid as the answer to the poor being the purported
root cause of environmental degradation.) If one ignores the mechanisms
that make people poor, it is easy to conclude that throwing money at the
problem is the answer to poverty. Sachs argues for more and better aid as
he lays out five mechanisms through which aid could turn Africa around,
from boosting agriculture to improving basic health care to providing education, electricity, and clean water. Through Sachs's efforts, aid has been
distributed in this manner to several "model" Kenyan villages.

We have seen this myth many times over the last half-century, as readers of this book are well aware. Indeed, in Walt Whitman Rostow's 1960
book *The Stages of Economic Growth: A Non-Communist Manifesto,* this senior
advisor to Presidents Kennedy and Johnson provided the intellectual rationale for the postwar aid effort. Rostow argued that "traditional societies"
needed aid and other external help to change their culture of primitiveness
and create the "preconditions for take-off" into modernization ("the age
of high mass consumption") by means of higher income levels.[22]

We do not dispute that under the *right* conditions and with the right
structure, aid can help mitigate disease and natural disasters—at least in the
short-term. But the reality is that its track record in reducing poverty was
as poor in Rostow's time as it is today. Former World Bank economist William Easterly calculates that rich countries "spent $568 billion (in today's
dollars) to end poverty in Africa" between 1960 and 2003, a period when
the number of poor in Africa rose steadily.[23]

In fact, there is ample evidence that financial aid often has a negative
impact on the alleviation of poverty. It is invariably channeled in such a way
as to widen the gap between the poor and the rest of society. Some years
ago, the American researchers Betsy Hartmann and James Boyce studied
an aid project that funded tubewells intended to bring irrigation water to

Bangladesh's small farmers. Time and time again, however, the tubewells ended up owned by the richest people in the village—effectively making them richer and more powerful, and leaving others (including the targeted beneficiaries) even poorer and less powerful than before.[24] The geographer Ben Wisner concluded that for aid to be considered successful there needed to be "a shift of power in favour of the disadvantaged group." But, said Wisner, "this effect is as rare as it is essential to [a project's] long-term sustainability and reproducibility."[25] Sachs's model Kenyan village aid project does not meet this criterion, and has been criticized for addicting farmers to expensive chemical inputs and requiring amounts of aid that would be impossible on a global scale.[26]

It would be more effective to put a halt to the outflow of financial resources from poor to rich countries through widespread debt cancellation. Far more money is sucked out of poor countries through debt service on the $2.5 trillion (as of 2005) owed to international lenders by 153 countries than comes in through aid, and stemming this outflow could free hundreds of billions of dollars for health care, education, and disease prevention.[27] (To be fair, Sachs is an advocate of debt cancellation.)

Myth # 4: After aid gets a country started on the development ladder, increased trade will propel it upward.

Here it is: the key Washington Consensus tenet (as we saw in Chapter 6, the one with the most resilience). As Sachs phrases it, "When the pre-conditions ... are in place, markets are powerful engines of development," given "the remarkable power of trade and investment" to catalyze "rapid economic growth" and combat poverty.[28] Friedman concurs: "Every law of economics tells us that if we ... promote greater and greater trade and integration, the global pie will grow wider and more complex."[29] Indeed, says Friedman, it is an "irrefutable fact that more open and competitive markets are the only sustainable vehicle for growing a nation out of poverty."[30] He then reiterates the arguments that the World Bank has imprinted on the minds of editorial writers everywhere, namely that China and South Asia reduced extreme poverty over the past fifteen years by opening their markets, while Africa kept its markets closed and poverty rose.[31]

How does the evidence stack up? After twenty-plus years of Washington Consensus dogma, it is, indeed, well past time to assess the evidence. First, does prying open markets help the poorest nations? During the 1990s, when market-opening policies were being pursued, the number of people living on less than a dollar a day in sub-Saharan Africa, Latin America and the Caribbean, and the Middle East increased.[32] One reason for this was that the prices paid to poor countries for their primary commodity exports during those years rose far more slowly than the prices of their manufactured imports. Indeed, according to a 2006 United Nations study, "the terms of trade of commodities (vis-à-vis manufactures) have declined, with the 2005 level 30% lower than the 1975–85 level."[33] Compounding this problem is the fact that when the World Bank and the IMF press poor countries to open their markets, imports tend to rise much faster than exports, with poor farmers often suffering the most. A 2005 study by Christian Aid concluded that "trade liberalization has cost sub-Saharan Africa US$272 billion over the past 20 years," roughly the amount that the region received in aid over this period.[34]

In addition, there is a solid body of evidence refuting the World Bank's heavily promoted research that market-opening policies lead to growth, research that Friedman cites as the source of his "irrefutable fact."[35] Mark Weisbrot of the Center for Economic and Policy Research has studied growth rates for poor countries in the 1980–2000 period, when most were pushed to open their markets, and he concludes that growth rates were substantially lower than during the 1960–1980 period, when markets were less open. Harvard economist Dani Rodrik's work on the relationship between trade liberalization and growth likewise refutes Friedman's supposed "irrefutable fact": "If anything, the evidence for the 1990s indicates a positive (but statistically insignificant) relationship between tariffs and economic growth." [36]

Extreme poverty did decline in China and India during the 1990s. But, as critics of neoliberalism have argued time and time again, neither country blindly followed neoliberal market-opening policies. Instead, each selectively and carefully opened some markets while leaving other markets to the exclusive domain of domestic firms. Beijing and New Delhi steered economic resources toward land reform, education, and other national goals. Today, it is harder to follow their path, given the opposition of the World Trade Organization and other market-opening institutions, but that does not change the fact that extreme poverty dropped in both, in large part as a result of government policy.[37] In the absence of government intervention, open markets tend to enrich large entrepreneurs and corporations, at the expense of the poor.

Lately, the alter-globalization movement has focused attention on what it calls the "Wal-Mart economy." By this it means a global economy of increasing mobility for global firms like Wal-Mart in the absence of effective protections for workers, small local businesses, and the environment. In listing the key "free-market strategies" that countries should adopt, Friedman includes "flexible labor laws."[38] This is Orwellian code language for undermining worker protections. In a Wal-Mart global economy, the accepted way for others to compete with cheap Chinese labor is through a race to the bottom in wages, working conditions, and government regulations.

Another critical problem that is too often ignored is that rapid trade and investment growth depend on heavy fossil fuel use that is accelerating a global climate crisis. Demand is skyrocketing in China and India. Indeed, the end of cheap energy, along with coming water shortages, could create more pressures to abandon neoliberal trade-expansion policies.[39] (We will return to this in Chapter 8.)

Myth #5: The only alternative to market-opening globalization is protectionism.

Once again, Washington Consensus backers put on blinders to the alternatives offered by the alter-globalization movement. In Friedman's words, the choice is "free trade" or "erect walls."[40] He concludes that the only way for rich countries like the United States to keep up as China and India surge ahead and grab millions of manufacturing and service jobs is to compete harder. (To get his daughters to do their homework, he reminds them that "people in China and India are starving for your jobs.")[41]

If Friedman or Sachs had lent a more sympathetic ear or even simply a more rigorous and objective research eye to what they simplistically refer to as the anti-globalization movement, they would have discovered that many citizen groups and governments reject both market opening at all costs and 1930s-style protectionism. And Friedman and Sachs would have discovered plenty of alternatives. The more properly termed alter-globalization movement draws from the ranks of union members, environmentalists, farmers, students, women, indigenous peoples, health activists, members of religious groups, researchers—and a growing number of elected officials, particularly in Latin America, where the electorates in Brazil, Argentina, Venezuela, Uruguay, and Bolivia have turned to political leaders who reject the Washington Consensus. In the conclusion of this book, we will turn to this alter-globalization movement and its goals, policies, and practices at the end of the first decade of the twenty-first century to demonstrate the depth and breadth of alternatives.

One could give Jeffrey Sachs and Thomas Friedman some credit for embracing the idea of ending poverty, and for bringing this issue to wider public notice. Yet, by basing their arguments on simplistic myths, they are attempting to hijack the development debate and resurrect key parts of the elite Washington Consensus. The well-meaning rock stars, government leaders, billionaires, and civil society organizations that have jumped on the Sachs/Friedman aid-and-trade bandwagon would do well to look deeper at the realities of "more trade" and "more aid;" they would do well

to look deeper at the alternatives offered by the alter-globalization movement. Only with such analytical reflection, only with such a refusal to accept facile answers and persistent myths, can the goal of "ending poverty"
actually be achieved.

Chapter 8

New Lenses on Development

This book, through its chapters of time travel, has examined the dynamic interplay of two sets of forces that have shaped the history of the developing world for the past three decades: the elite backers of the Washington Consensus and the citizen organizations of the alter-globalization movement.

We have walked you through the events and forces behind the birth and surge of the Washington Consensus in the 1980s, the subsequent rise and fall of the Consensus in the 1990s, and the attempts to resuscitate parts of the Consensus in the 2000s. We have brought you to a point where, standing at the end of the first decade of the twenty-first century, we can confidently state that the reign of the Washington Consensus is over.

Simultaneously, the book has charted the emergence of the alter-globalization movement from it roots in the 1970s to its powerful coalescence over the past two decades. We have watched this movement grow from a few citizen groups in a few countries to broad sectors across many countries. We have chronicled the evolution of this movement from a largely defensive movement that critiqued and opposed neoliberalism to a movement on the offensive that is implementing alternatives on the ground.

In our time travel, we have analyzed the dynamics of these two powerful forces of history and their interaction. But we have done so not merely as tour guides taking you back in time to watch this history unfold. We have traveled with you to share the perspectives and insights gained from our three decades of work in the South and North.

Building on these chapters, we turn now to the current and future trajectories of these two sets of opposing interests. First, we explore the key developments on the global scene that are influencing the next phase of the development debate and reality. Second, we look more deeply into the alter-globalization movement in terms of alternatives in action. Finally, we build from the analytical lenses we have used during our time travel to leave you, the reader, with key questions to ask as you assess new institutions and new proposals—be it the newly launched Bank of the South or new proposals for debt relief.

The Changing Landscape

Chapter 6 chronicled the cracking of the Consensus, and Chapter 7 the attempts to extend the life of the Consensus. Now, some years later, we are at a moment in history where the chances of resuscitation are even weaker. Various phenomena account for this, three of which we highlight below. None should come as a surprise, inasmuch as you have witnessed parts of these stories in preceding chapters, but all three now have reached stages that bring us to a new moment of history.

Crises at the World Bank, IMF, and WTO

In mid-2007, a *New York Times* article started with words that would have been unimaginable in the mainstream press even a half-decade earlier: "[T]he entire international economic architecture established after World War II—the World Bank, the International Monetary Fund and what is now called the World Trade Organization—is buckling under the weight of globalization, trade disputes and the ambitions of rising economic power in Asia and elsewhere."[1]

Why are the multilateral financial and trade institutions that have played such a prominent role in this book as the key public levers of the Washington Consensus so significantly weakened? As chronicled in these pages, adverse impacts of their policies—and the arrogance and recalcitrance of these institutions—over these past decades have sparked public opposition around the world. This became even more widespread after their spectacular failure in the Asian financial crisis.[2] In addition to their crises of credibility and legitimacy, the Bank and Fund are now experiencing financial difficulties as countries bypass their resources and turn instead to China, Venezuela, and other new donors for loans, often less encumbered by onerous conditions.

The World Bank, desperate to keep middle-income clients from which it earns income, has announced plans to reduce interest rates on its loans to them. The Bank liberally deploys the rhetoric of its critics, from poverty reduction to more consultation with the public to an acknowledgment of the necessity of governments. Its structural adjustment loans have been relabeled "anti-poverty loans" and "development policy support" loans. But those changes are largely cosmetic. A report by the European Network on Debt and Development, for example, discovered that—contrary to the Bank's claim that Washington Consensus polices no longer dominated its conditionality—the Bank "is still making heavy use of [such] economic policy conditionality, especially in sensitive areas such as privatisation and liberalisation."[3] In addition, the Bank has suffered stinging external critiques about the objectivity and reliability of its research—especially that related to economic globalization and its purported undisputed proof that liberalization causes economic growth.[4]

In 2007, the World Bank's self-advertisement that it stands with the poor and against corruption came under particularly heavy public ridicule during a protracted internal dispute (turned media frenzy) over then president Paul Wolfowitz's overly generous pay packages for his partner (a World Bank employee) and his top deputies (most, like himself, neoconservatives who came out of the Bush administration). This scandal heightened the criticism of U.S. power in the Bank, the inequitable voting structure, and the sixty-year-old "tradition" whereby the U.S. government selects the Bank president and Europeans pick the head of the IMF.

The International Monetary Fund is in even more dire shape than the Bank. After the disasters of the Asian financial crisis demonstrated the Fund's ineptitude, the Fund's next moment of truth began in 2001–2002, when its longtime model client Argentina faced economic collapse, defaulted on many of its debts, changed course as it rejected IMF prescriptions, and went on to grow rapidly in the ensuing years. As *USA Today* phrased it, "by defying the conventional economic wisdom. . . . and shunning the . . . International Monetary Fund," Argentina became "Exhibit A for those who doubt globalization's one-size-fits-all policy prescription."[5] Other IMF clients became so keen to get out of the Fund's grasp that they are paying back in full and in advance. Indeed, in 2007, the bulk of the Fund's outstanding loans were to Turkey, leading *The Economist* to call it the "Turkish Monetary Fund."[6] The irony of the longtime lender-of-last-resort and manager of financial crises being in its own financial crisis has not been lost on observers.

Thus, both the Bank and Fund stand today as significantly weakened institutions, but both are desperately trying to regain credibility, legitimacy, and power. In 2007, in a shrewd move, the Bush administration chose Washington Consensus backer and former U.S. trade representative Robert Zoellick to head the Bank. Zoellick already has at least one victory for the Bank under his belt, having successfully convinced governments to put new resources into its lending facility for the very poorest nations (the International Development Association). More controversially, he has broached the idea of accepting contributions from corporations and foundations—a move that would call into question the public character of the Bank. And the Bank is attempting to place itself center stage as the public institution to address the climate crisis, notwithstanding the hypocrisy that it still pours billions of dollars annually into fossil-fuel loans.[7]

So too is the IMF trying to remake itself. Soon after Dominique Strauss-Kahn took over as IMF managing director in 2007, he admitted that the institution is struggling with relevance and mandate ("[I]t is a factory to produce paper") and announced plans to deal with the Fund's financial shortfall, in part by a large-scale cut of staff. Fund officials are deeply worried that when the next financial crisis erupts, poorer nations might bypass the Fund altogether and turn to emerging regional institutions for short-term finance. As Strauss-Kahn acknowledged to the *Wall Street Journal:* "The legitimacy of the IMF relies upon the capacity to have everybody on board, including those countries with which there have been problems in the past."[8]

This recent weakening of the Bank and Fund is correlated with a weakened ability to use the Third World debt crisis to impose Washington Consensus conditions on poorer nations—a decided change from a quarter-century ago. Indeed, many larger and faster growing poorer nations have escaped Bank and Fund surveillance by building up foreign exchange reserves and finding alternative sources of finance. But, as we have seen earlier in this book, one has to be careful not to generalize. Many smaller, indebted, poorer nations, especially in Africa, are still burdened with external debt and remain dependent on Bank and Fund loans and are subject to their strictures. That is especially true of countries dependent on importing increasingly expensive fossil fuels and food. Even here, however, there are notable exceptions: Some of the poorest countries have qualified for debt relief (but, as noted in Chapter 6, with conditionality attached); others have found alternative sources of funding (witness Bolivia).

And some have dared to challenge Bank dictums. In a case that is subjecting the Bank to criticism and embarrassment akin to what the Fund faced on Argentina, Malawi has reacted to a crisis in its domestic corn crop and impending famine by reinstating fertilizer subsidies that the Bank had pressed it to slash. The result? In 2007, Malawi is not only feeding its own population but also "exporting hundreds of thousands of tons of corn to Zimbabwe."[9]

Additionally, the global trade body, the WTO, stands on the verge of failure to complete a new round of trade rules. Negotiations have broken down many times since the 2001 launch of the so-called Development Round (or Doha Round), including in late 2007. What is clear is the inability of the United States, Europe, and Japan to control trade negotiations as they once did. Part of the challenge comes from the strengthened voice of some Southern governments. Part is from the growing sophistication of civil society groups in critiquing the proposals. The WTO's credibility as an institution representing interests of rich and poor alike is also under broad attack, with growing acknowledgement by insiders and outsiders that the likely gains from a new trade round are less than previously hyped, and that most of the gains will likely stay in the North. A Tufts University study brought attention to World Bank data showing a "likely scenario" from the negotiations of Southern "gains" of only $6.7 billion versus Northern gains of $31.7 billion—or, in more stark terms, an average of "less than a penny a day for those in the developing world."[10]

The waning power of the Bank and Fund and the paralysis of the WTO negotiations have re-created some of the policy space that the Consensus had taken away. The debate is out in the open; more are acknowledging that the emperor has no clothes.

Planetary Environmental Crises

As we traveled back in time to the gelling of market fundamentalism, we noted John Williamson's remark that the Consensus had "almost nothing to do with the environmental question," local or global. Those blinders are proving exceedingly short-sighted as the environmental limits of export-led neoliberal policies are becoming harder to ignore. Part of this is the scaling up of the local environmental costs we detailed in Chapters 3 and 4. The rapid increase in trade and cross-border investment inherent to the Consensus vision requires massive amounts of fossil fuel for ocean and jet transport. Together, the industrialization of agriculture and manufacturing and the transport requirements for such exports have accelerated the release of greenhouse gas emissions.

As awareness of local and planetary environmental limits grows, so too is another nail hammered in the Consensus's coffin. Indeed, the increasing acknowledgment of environmental constraints turns the economic globalization agenda on its head; a key policy issue for countries in the near future may well be how to reduce trade while maintaining healthy standards of living. Here too, of course, some Consensus backers are rejecting this conclusion as they attempt to resurrect old myths to suggest that market mechanisms such as carbon trading and corporate innovations in biofuels, nuclear power, and "clean coal" can solve the crises.

Opposition in Latin America and Beyond

This book has charted the rise in Latin America of resistance to Consensus policies as they failed to deliver promised economic results, and as social and environmental disasters spread. In recent years, this resistance moved into the electoral arena, with citizens voting into office politicians who promise to reverse the course of neoliberalism (as it is typically called there). The tally of countries that have moved in this direction includes Venezuela, Ecuador, Bolivia, Chile, Argentina, Brazil, Nicaragua, Uruguay, and Paraguay. (Among others, Mexico, Peru, and Costa Rica almost joined this trend when anti-neoliberal challengers in recent presidential elections lost by small margins.)[11] Venezuela, one of the world's largest oil producers, has translated rising oil prices into new clout on the global stage, with President Hugo Chavez openly challenging the United States and neoliberalism and financing alternatives.

But the point is not merely the presence or leadership of Hugo Chavez, although it is more convenient for Consensus backers to pretend this is the case. The key point is that the synergy of so many countries pursuing new paths at the same moment has created a global pole of governmental opposition to neoliberalism to supplement the citizen backlash. Exactly how this will play out is unclear: These nations fall along a political continuum, with Venezuela professing a "socialist" path to development, Argentina openly challenging its creditors, Bolivia and Ecuador pursuing bold alternatives on both the social and environmental level, Paraguay initiating pro-poor policies, and Chile, Uruguay, and Brazil still pursuing many Washington Consensus policies. But again, what is clear is that these nations together pose a significant challenge to Consensus thinking.

What else should the reader keep watching to follow this changing debate and landscape? Outside of Latin America, two countries that perhaps bear the closest watching are China and India. As noted earlier in this book, both have been growing at rates that outstrip almost all other countries for over a decade, with many attendant plusses and minuses. While economic growth is creating billionaires in both and incomes are rising for many, each is deluged with rising inequality and multiple environmental and social ills. As China has assumed the mantle of the world's top manufacturer (producing half the world's cameras and a third of its TVs), it is now consuming half the world's steel and concrete, and it is slated to build roughly half the world's buildings over the next ten years. In the process, it has generated a third of the world's garbage annually, despoiled its rivers and lakes, fueled rampant illegal logging in neighboring countries, and become the largest emitter of greenhouse gases in the world, provoking thousands of local environmental protests.[12]

Although Washington Consensus die-hards still try to claim that China's and India's "success" is due to neoliberal policies, China and India continue to pursue strategies that involve an active government role in steering resources toward particular sectors. Rather than poster children of the Consensus, these two giants—with all their warts—are examples of governments placing checks on market forces. China is also becoming a huge force in the world of trade, investment, and aid as it turns to Africa for oil and minerals, to Latin America for soybeans and other agricultural commodities, and to the rest of the globe as a market for its tens of millions of metal containers filled with computers, toys, clothing, and other goods.[13] And so China and India bear watching closely—not only in terms of their evolving development models and growing environmental movements internally but also in terms of what role they decide to play in global economic institutions. Where those governments position themselves in the debate could greatly affect the outcomes.

In 2008, it was the soaring price of food and of some raw materials that grabbed media and public attention. As most accounts have it, China's and India's insatiable demand for minerals and agricultural commodities is among the contributing factors. At the same time, the exhaustion of easy-to-extract petroleum (i.e., the advent of so-called peak oil) and the Iraq war put upward pressure on fuel prices—which, in turn, boosts the cost of fertilizers and pesticides. To this mix, add the competition of biofuels with food crops for land. The result: skyrocketing food prices, "food riots" in a number of countries, and devastating hunger. Or, at least, that is the story as typically told.

But, our time travel in this book gives us a deeper, historical understanding of the creation of poverty and of hunger: of how the decades of World Bank and other neoliberal policies commercialized and globalized agriculture, de-prioritized production of food for local consumption, uprooted small-scale farmers from their land, and increased the vulnerability of significant portions of rural and urban populations, while making countries food-import dependent. To the extent that the food crisis of the late 2000s comes to be understood as having roots in Consensus policies, so too will this further delegitimate neoliberalism.

The food crisis, developments in China and India, and the three new challenges to the Consensus outlined above reinforce the criticisms outlined in the seven preceding chapters. But, let us be very clear: Market fundamentalism has not disappeared. There are still some stalwart defenders of the Consensus, and Sachs's and Friedman's new offshoots of the religion still attract converts. There are some who still feel that markets are the sole route to prosperity; these individuals argue for minor tinkering of the Consensus, but want to leave it largely intact. Nor is it easy for Southern governments to break with the Consensus or its institutions: Brazil, led by a former metalworker and union leader, has shown how hard it is to shake neoliberal policies as his government has continued to pursue export-oriented industrialization and agribusiness. Moreover, there are still many poorer nations (particularly in Africa) that remain mired in debt and dependent on international financial institutions, with seemingly little space to maneuver away from Consensus prescriptions. The World Bank, IMF, and WTO desperately search for redemption and new roles. Global corporations remain powerful actors on global stages; many look to expand sales by draping themselves in eco-friendly rhetoric.

These caveats notwithstanding, the public institutions that were the main enforcers of the Washington Consensus are in crisis, and the legitimacy of market fundamentalism is severely diminished. The renewed energy that the Consensus received from the terrorist attacks of September 11 proved to be relatively short-lived, weakened in part by the ineptness of the George W. Bush administration's overall response to terrorism. Almost none of the participants in the development debate of today would argue that the market alone is enough. The curtain has been pulled away to expose the inflated pretensions of neoliberalism; the little man who was the Wizard of Oz is revealed for all who are willing to look.

Significantly, debate has even found its way back to academic economists. As the *New York Times* phrased it in a title to a 2007 article: "In Economics Departments, a Growing Will to Debate Fundamental Assumptions." In that article, Professor Robert Reich, a former cabinet minister in the Clinton administration, explained: "Economists can't pretend that the consensus for free markets and free trade that existed 30 years ago is still here."[14]

As we stated at the start of this chapter, standing at the end of the first decade of the twenty-first century, we can confidently state that the era of market fundamentalism is over. In this period—after the eclipse of the old era and yet before a clear unfolding of a new era—it is foolhardy to write with any sense of assuredness about the future. We are in a period of open contestation for ideas, for clarity, for power. But, as we have shown in this first part of our concluding chapter, we are decidedly in a new era. We are witnessing the return of the debate about development, a debate that we have called for throughout our travels in this book. This, however, is not simply a return to the development debates of the pre-Consensus years, vibrant as those debates were. The new debates also reflect the new moment in history: Given the strength of the alter-globalization movement and the experience of the Washington Consensus decades, this time around the debates dig more deeply, to the fundamental questions: What is development? What is the role of government, and of other sectors of society? Whom should development serve?

Daily, new forces rise to challenge the Consensus and create alternatives to it. In the next section of this chapter, we move to sketch the contours of the opposing forces, and the alternatives emerging all over the world. This too is part of what marks our entry into a new historical moment. No longer can Consensus backers claim that "there is no alternative."

Alternatives in Action

Let us examine the alter-globalization movement—or, more correctly, this movement of movements—more closely to see where it stands today. Although there are many different proposals, most alternative projects have as a common starting point a redefinition of development. Most groups in the movement prioritize the fulfillment of people's basic social, economic, cultural, and political rights. They measure progress in terms of the improved health and well-being of children, families, communities, democracy, and the natural environment.[15] Rather than a linear "take-off," development in this view involves the redistribution of political power and wealth downward. A team of researchers from richer and poorer countries (including the authors) affiliated with the International Forum on Globalization worked collectively—discussing and debating—to distill the alter-globalization movement's principles in *Alternatives to Economic Globalization*: democracy, ecological sustainability, subsidiarity (favoring local production), protection of common resources (such as air, water, and parks), human rights, food security, equity, and cultural and biological diversity.[16]

These goals are important, but part of what is exciting is that alternatives in action—which build on the above principles—abound. In the introduction to this book, we outlined how in the 1960s and 1970s, alternatives took shape at local (Tanzania's self-reliant villages), national (import-substitution industrialization by Brazil and other countries), regional (the common markets), and global (New International Economic Order) levels. The same is true today, although there is a crucial difference between that era of debate and different paths of development, and the period we are entering now: the actors involved. In the 1960s and 1970s, the key actors pressing for change were largely Third World governments, energized by key intellectuals with a clear framework for change. Today, the dynamism for change is coming much more from social movements and citizen organizations, which are both creating alternatives and pressing governments and global institutions for change. In the words of Oscar Olivera, the Bolivian activist who has led several campaigns to keep municipal water systems out of the hands of global corporations, "[T]he true transformational power of life resides in people's capacity for organization and mobilization."[17]

A brief sampling of the current initiatives at the local, national, regional, and global levels is enough to give a sense of the breadth and depth of this activity.

Local

Local governments, under pressure from citizen groups in many parts of the world, are encouraging family farms, innovative worker-owned enterprises, green building and environment-sustaining design, and the revitalization of public transportation and utilities. Curitiba, Brazil—a city the size of Houston—has been transformed into the "greenest" city in that country, by providing incentives for public transportation, bike paths, nonpolluting industries, and massive recycling. In Bolivia, Ghana, Nigeria, and elsewhere, grassroots movements are reversing the two-decade trend of selling key public utilities, such as municipal water systems, to global firms. In Cochabamba, Bolivia, a consortium that included the international giant Bechtel was forced out in favor of a local-ownership model by Olivera and his local groups. In Porto Alegre, Brazil, participatory budgeting processes in place since 1989 involve large numbers of local people in setting government spending priorities. In Guatemala, Nicaragua, Mexico, and Cuba, mobile teams of farmer-technicians from the "Campesino a Campesino" movement share innovative sustainable agriculture practices—protecting the environment, producing food, and improving the incomes of hundreds of thousands of smallholders.[18]

National

At the national level, governments of many poorer countries are pressing for changes in global trade rules that will given them more "space" to set their own priorities as well as their own industrial and agriculture policies, such as favoring domestic farms and firms over global corporations. Brazil and Argentina, for example, are among those countries that have gained independence from the conditionalities of the International Monetary Fund by paying back their loans in full. This has allowed them to give more attention to social, environmental, and equity considerations over purely aggregate economic goals.

Under pressure from an invigorated citizenry, the Lula government in Brazil oversaw a three-year decline in deforestation rates in the Amazon (through 2007) via a combination of measures, including stricter regulations, arrests of illegal loggers, and the creation of protected areas—although no one should have illusions about the power of the forces attempting to counter these measures. The Bolivian government has renegotiated contracts with foreign oil and natural gas firms, generating more than $1.5 billion in extra revenues in 2006 and 2007 that the government aims to channel into reducing poverty, particularly for the country's majority indigenous population and the elderly.[19]

In the Philippines, Ecuador, South Africa, and several other poorer countries, slow but significant progress is being made in gaining legal recognition of the ancestral domain rights of indigenous peoples. In addition, a growing number of countries are establishing community–based natural resource management systems that devolve varying degrees of local authority to indigenous and other local communities.

Perhaps more surprising is that, in the wake of the Asian financial crisis, more and more people in the once export-oriented "success" story of Thailand are becoming attracted to what is called the "sufficiency economy" paradigm advocated by the Thai king; the Thai "sufficiency economy" movement has anti-export economy and anti-globalization overtones. As Walden Bello explains, the sufficiency economy "is an inward-looking strategy that stresses self-reliance at the grassroots and the creation of strong ties among domestic economic networks."[20] Among the development successes noted by the UN Development Program are those in the poor northeastern part of the country where more than 100,000 farmers have joined a network to shift land from cash crops to rice, and to help one another with community enterprises, health care, and environmental conservation.[21]

As the above examples suggest, many citizen groups and governments are also rethinking aid and open markets, which neoliberalism so single-mindedly promoted. In the Philippines and several other countries, citizen groups have set up innovative structures to channel aid money to endow foundations, which in turn fund small-scale, grassroots projects that often help local groups control and manage forest and fishing resources in a sustainable manner. On the debt front, Ecuador appears to have launched a significant initiative in 2007 by setting up a National Debt Audit Commission tasked with "establish[ing] the illegitimacy and illegality of the debts claimed of the Ecuadorean government and to recommend measures for securing justice and reparation."[22]

The "fair trade movement" seeks to bypass global corporations and set up alternative trading arrangements that discourage sweatshop working conditions and environmental destruction while ensuring that benefits remain local. This includes product labeling initiatives that let consumers know that rugs have been produced without child labor (RugMark), T-shirts have been sewn by workers paid a living wage (No Sweat), and wood products have been made from timber that was harvested in a sustainable manner (Forest Stewardship Council). Numerous outlets—from Equal Exchange in Massachusetts to Dean's Beans—now sell "fair trade" coffee from Latin America, Africa, and Asia that has been certified by a third-party monitor. There is even fair trade music.

Regional

This book has charted the evolution of regional institutions from the more insular trade blocs of the 1960s and 1970s to the Washington Consensus agreements such as NAFTA, which opened markets within a region to the large corporations from member countries. Today, there are other alternatives to the "free-trade, free-investment-flow" model. The European Union, for example, offers a model of regional integration in which poor member states such as Ireland and Portugal were aided by carefully targeted resource transfers and the setting of common (and high) labor and social rules.[23]

In Latin America, the Venezuelan government is earmarking part of its surging oil revenues to fund new regional integration initiatives as a counterweight to the corporate-led integration proposals of the United States. For example, through the Bolivarian Alternative for the Americas and the Caribbean (ALBA), Venezuela, Cuba, and Bolivia are promoting new forms of economic cooperation, beginning with the sharing of resources such as oil in exchange for Cuban health care expertise.[24]

In terms of regional alternatives to the global financial architecture, the creation of a Banco del Sur (Bank of the South) by seven Latin American governments in December 2007 attracted a great deal of attention. Government officials from Argentina, Bolivia, Brazil, Ecuador, Paraguay, Uruguay, and Venezuela set up the development bank with a one-country, one-vote structure that differs markedly from the World Bank's weighted voting structure.[25]

On the other side of the globe, in Asia, one also finds initiatives to create new regional financial institutions emerging in the wake of the 1997 Asian financial crisis. Notable is the so-called Chiang Mai Initiative, a framework for regional financial cooperation launched by finance ministers from most East Asian and Southeast Asian nations as a regional mechanism to avoid future crises in place of the IMF. The Chiang Mai Initiative allows pairs of countries to lend each other money at favorable terms were a financial crisis to erode the value of a specific currency. Members can borrow condition-free up to a certain level through this initiative—although above that amount, IMF-style conditions kick in.[26]

Global

With the one-size-fits-all policies of the World Trade Organization, the World Bank, and the IMF increasingly being questioned by citizen groups and governments alike, there are an array of proposals—and debates—to replace some of their functions with institutions whose purposes range from raising and stabilizing commodity prices, to acting as a lender of last resort by providing short-term loans without conditions in crisis situations, to offering menus of policy advice. While these could well be the regional bodies described above, there are also proposals for global institutions. Organizations such as the International Forum on Globalization and the Workshop on International Regulations have laid out the contours of alternative global trade and finance organizations that advance such principles as democratic self-determination, balanced trade, fair commodity prices, and open access to information and knowledge.[27] Such regional and global trade bodies could preserve vital policy space for national governments.

So too does removing the debt burden remain a focus. A dynamic global campaign came together in the 1990s under the biblical call for "Jubilee" debt cancellation. As we noted in Chapter 6, the campaign gained momentum as the Bank and Fund created their Heavily Indebted Poor Countries (HIPC) debt initiative in the late 1990s. As of early 2008, the Jubilee campaign helped to create the pressure that resulted in the Group of Eight rich countries offering twenty-three poorer countries debt relief—cancellation of 100 percent of IMF, World Bank, African Development Bank, and InterAmerican Development Bank debts. Jubilee campaigners are now pushing for debt cancellation for a much larger group of countries, for an audit of odious and illegitimate debts (to identify which debts should automatically be cancelled), for elimination of harmful free-market policy conditions that still accompany debt relief, and for a new framework for responsible lending in the future to avoid a new debt crisis and the creation of new odious debts.[28]

Other parts of the alter-globalization movement have become vocal participants in global negotiations to confront the climate and natural-resource crises. They have tabled proposals to replace the Kyoto Protocol (the global agreement to reduce greenhouse gas emissions) with new arrangements to advance core alter-globalization principles through what campaigners are calling "global climate justice." These proposals include deeper binding targets to reduce greenhouse gas emissions by a minimum average of at least 80 percent below 1990 levels by 2050, while ensuring that richer nations, and the richer segments within all nations, bear the greatest burden of adjustment. In global meetings on climate (such as the December 2007 negotiations in Bali, Indonesia), parts of the alter-globalization movement have called on governments to create new global mechanisms that would help nations keep fossil fuels in the ground, finance North-South resource transfers, cut back oil production and consumption, advance rights to clean water, and protect forests, fisheries, biodiversity, fragile ecosystems, and endangered species. On water, for example, a global network has proposed a UN covenant that would establish the right to water and would prohibit global corporate control of municipal water systems.[29]

In essence, many of these groups are proposing a paradigm shift that would replace the consumption-oriented, high-growth model with a low-carbon, low-growth economy where a more equitable income distribution would allow for a rise in the living standards of the poor. Techno-fixes such as nuclear power, mega-hydro, or carbon sequestration and storage would no longer do; rather, large-scale changes in consumption and production would have to be made quickly, given the small window of opportunity. Another way of looking at this is that climate change is providing citizen groups with an opportunity to advance the alter-globalization movement's alternative development and equity agenda.

The above sampling of initiatives and proposals is not meant to be exhaustive, but rather to offer a flavor of the dynamism and innovation of the moment. They demonstrate the wealth of alternatives in the twenty-first century.

Questions for a New Era

Together, all of the policies, initiatives, institutions, and proposals mentioned above add up to something new. As the world enters the post–Washington Consensus era, many more new proposals and initiatives will be launched all around the world—by governments, by the private sector, by civil society. The list of alternatives will change. We will study these proposals, and we urge you to as well. As you have undoubtedly gathered by journeying with us, our experiences have taught us to be skeptical of most of what comes from elites in the North and South or from the so-called development establishment. And it has taught us to be wary of the front page newspaper articles that announce new quick fixes, be it on debt relief, more aid, new trade pacts, or any other subject. Even the most promising proposals should be viewed with a critical eye.

One must refuse to accept easy answers and persistent myths. One must look at the connections—from global to local and from local to global—by wearing what we like to think of as multifaceted development lenses. That is, in essence, what we have done throughout our travels. At each of our stops in history, we have used these lenses to look more deeply. Indeed, these lenses can become the frame through which new events and proposals can be filtered.

But let us transform them now into a series of questions meant to serve as guideposts to assess future proposals.[30] At the outset of the book, we asked the core questions: "What is development? And development for and by whom?" More specific subquestions follow logically: Whose proposal is it? Does it conflate "development" with aggregate economic growth? Does it conflate the interests of the poor and marginalized with aggregate "Southern" interests at a nation-state or elite level? What would it look like from the ground up, through the eyes of the marginalized populations? Who would ultimately benefit from it—not just in a given static moment in time but dynamically over the years? Is it designed in such a way as to ensure that the wealthier segments of society will not reap the bulk of the benefits? Does it strengthen community control over their resources— economic, political, social, and environmental? Does it shift ownership away from large or global corporations toward those on the ground? Does the proposal help shift power toward the dispossessed and marginalized?

Put on these new development lenses and apply such questions whenever you hear about a new proposal. For example, take the new Banco del Sur that we mention above as a regional initiative. The easy reaction is to applaud it as an alternative whose very existence will weaken the public institutions that brought neoliberalism to much of the South. But while the creation of this new Latin American bank is indeed another manifestation of the end of the Washington Consensus era, which should be applauded on that level, it is too soon to applaud it as a new path to development redefined. What, for example, if it ends up lending primarily for fossil-fuel energy production and distribution (for example, pipelines) in Latin America?

Indeed, alter-globalization groups have appropriately greeted the Banco del Sur with guarded support. As several hundred Latin American social movements and networks wrote to the presidents of the seven nations that initiated the bank in December 2007: "It is our conviction that a new South-South financial entity should be focused not only on going beyond the negative experiences of economic opening ... but also beyond the well-known non-democratic, non-transparent, regressive and discredited behavior of [existing] multilateral bodies such as the World Bank, ... the IADB [InterAmerican Development Bank] and the IMF." Rather, they continued, the Banco del Sur should promote "a new development framework" via its lending. They also requested that the Banco del Sur be open to "the participation of citizen organizations and social movements, not only in the development of its original architecture but also in financial and operational decision making, and in the monitoring of the use given to the funds awarded."[31] In other words, this segment of civil society is asking that the Banco del Sur be set up to internalize the answers to the questions of "what is development" and "development by whom and for whom" in its very structure and purpose.

Or take an initiative that emerged in Ecuador in 2007. The country has untapped oil reserves located in the heart of the Ecuadorean Amazon, a region that is not only one of the most biologically rich in the world but is also home to indigenous peoples who depend on the land for survival.[32] Ecuador's government responded to pleas by those indigenous inhabitants to stop oil exploitation by offering a new proposal to leave one-fifth of the nation's oil reserves in the ground if Northern donors paid roughly half of what Ecuador would have received by selling the oil. The government's rationale behind this proposal seems logical: Since Ecuador is a poorer and heavily indebted country that largely depends on oil revenues to fund government social programs and other services, it should be compensated and assisted by the international community for such environmental efforts that would benefit non-Ecuadoreans as well.

On first blush, this sounds intriguing, perhaps even bold and laudable. But, again, we really do not know unless we dig more deeply. This proposal might or might not help ordinary Ecuadoreans, the indigenous inhabitants, or the planet depending on answers to the kinds of questions that emerge when we view the proposal through our development lenses: Who would receive the Northern aid—the government or the indigenous communities? Will the aid mechanism be set up so that the indigenous communities are empowered? Are these communities involved in the design of the aid flows? That is, who gets the money and who gets the power?

We end our book by raising these questions so that, as you glance at newspaper headlines of new global initiatives, or as you curl up with the next Sachs or Friedman book, or as you travel to the next World Social Forum, you do so with your eyes open wide and your critical thinking engaged. Put on those development lenses. Ask questions about every new initiative. As billions of dollars of Chinese aid flow into Africa, ask the questions. As debt relief is extended to Liberia and other countries, ask the questions. As the World Bank proposes a facility to pay nations to preserve their forests, ask the questions.[33] As a new administration in the United States announces a new aid or trade initiative, ask the questions.

We write this book with the hope that never again should development policies reign that have not been shaped and tested on the ground. Never again should a decidedly elite "consensus" tilted toward the benefit of the few be able to masquerade as a consensus of the world's majority. We write this book with the conviction that an informed public asking the right questions will add to the vibrancy of the development debate and will enhance the chances of the future looking more like the one envisioned by the alter-globalization movement. We hope you will join us in those debates and add your questions.

Over the last thirty years, the world has lived through a devastating development era and is on the threshold of a new one. In this book, we have traveled through time to highlight the main components of this old era, that of the Washington Consensus. We followed its rapid ascent and its slow decline. We visited with its victims and charted their coalescence into a powerful worldwide alter-globalization movement.

We hope that this book serves as a warning of the dangers of any overarching development orthodoxy. One size never fits all. Each community, each nation, must choose its own path and must have the maximum space—economic, environmental, social, political—to make those choices.

Our collaborative travels are over for now. But we hope that you keep traveling—back in time as well as in the present—to watch this new era unfold. Touch ground. And, keep asking: What would any proposal mean for people like Abraham and that indigenous community in the southern Philippines? What is development? How does one make it happen? And, development for whom and by whom?

Notes

1. We write mindful of the distaste the term "development" has for some. We believe, however, that to frame the word "development" as we have in these questions makes it clear that we are not defining development as economic growth, or as modernization, or in such senses as suggested by U.S. president Truman when he ushered in the "program of development" in 1949. Whether the challenge is to redefine "development" or to use another term as that redefined goal, we see the essence of the quest as similar.

For further reading on what Wolfgang Sachs calls the "tainted ... glasses ... in the prevailing development discourse," see Wolfgang Sachs, ed., *The Development Dictionary: A Guide to Knowledge as Power* (London: Zed, 1992) (Sachs's quotation is from p. 5); Arturo Escobar, *Encountering Development: The Making and Unmaking of the Third World* (Princeton: Princeton University Press, 1995); and Gustavo Esteva, with M. S. Prakash, "Beyond Development, What?" *Development in Practice* vol. 8, no. 3 (August 1998): 280–296.

2. George Soros, *On Globalization* (New York: PublicAffairs, 2002), pp. 4–10.

3. The ten areas of consensus in terms of neoliberal, free-market policies, as noted by Williamson, are these: "fiscal discipline" (that is, policies to combat fiscal deficits); "public expenditure priorities" (cutting expenditures through the removal of subsidies and the like); "tax reform"; "financial liberalization" (moving toward market-determined interest rates); competitive "exchange rates"; "trade liberalization" (replacing licenses with tariffs and reducing tariffs); "foreign direct investment" (that is, removing barriers); "privatization"; "deregulation" (of impediments to competition); and "property rights." See John Williamson,

The Progress of Policy Reform in Latin America, Policy Analyses in International Economics, no. 28 (Washington, D.C.: Institute for International Economics, January 1990).

4. Williamson, *Progress of Policy Reform in Latin America,* p. 9.

5. John Williamson, "Democracy and the 'Washington Consensus,'" *World Development* vol. 21, no. 8 (1993): 1329.

6. Williamson, *Progress of Policy Reform,* p. 83.

7. See *Philippines: Repression and Resistance—Permanent Peoples' Tribunal Session on the Philippines* (Utrecht, The Netherlands: Philippine-European Solidarity Center-Komite ng Sambayanang Pilipino [PESC-KSP], 1980).

8. As you will discover as you read on, we believe that the term that most accurately reflects this movement is "alter-globalization," since the movement encompasses both alternatives to the current economic globalization and alternative ways to globalize economically. We find the term "anti-globalization movement" faulty and misleading, since it suggests that the movement is *against* any forms of globalization. For Richard Falk's early use of the term "globalization from below" (which was later picked up by Jeremy Brecher and others), see Richard Falk, "The Making of Global Citizenship," in *Global Visions: Beyond the New World Order,* eds. Jeremy Brecher, John Brown Childs, and Jill Cutler (Boston: South End Press, 1993).

To follow academic work on these movements, see the journal *Globalizations,* and the work of its editor Barry Gills. See also Jan Aart Scholte, *Globalization: A Critical Introduction* (New York: Palgrave Macmillan, 2005), and James Mittelman, *The Globalization Syndrome: Transformation and Resistance* (Princeton: Princeton University Press, 2000).

9. See, for example, Jai Sen, Anita Anand, Arturo Escobar, and Peter Waterman, eds., *World Social Forum: Challenging Empires* (New Delhi: Viveka Foundation, 2004); and Jackie Smith et al., *Global Democracy and the World Social Forums* (Boulder, Colo.: Paradigm Publishers, 2008).

10. Dean Acheson, *Present at the Creation: My Years in the State Department* (New York: W. W. Norton, 1969).

11. For more details on this era of history, see Robin Broad, Part II: "The Historical Context" in *Global Backlash: Citizen Initiatives for a Just World Economy* (Boulder, Colo.: Rowman and Littlefield, 2002), pp. 63–114.

12. Quoted in Ramesh Ponnuru, "'We Are All Clueless Now': The Eclipse of Economies—Neither Party Has a Clear Economic Policy," *National Review,* November 8, 1999.

13. Three books that cover the history of these debates over the government role in development are Ha-Joon Chang, *Bad Samaritans: The Myth of Free Trade and the Secret History of Capitalism* (New York: Bloomsbury Press, 2008); James Fallows, *Looking at the Sun: The Rise of the New East Asian Economic and Political System* (New York: Vintage, 1994); and Ann Tickner, *Self-Reliance Versus Power Politics: American and Indian Experiences in Building Nation-States* (New York: Columbia University Press, 1987).

14. For an excellent recapitulation of structuralism in original texts, see Raul

Prebisch, *The Economic Development of Latin America and Its Principle Problems* (New York: UN Department of Economic Affairs, 1950); Albert Hirschmann, *The Strategy of Economic Development* (Hartford, Conn.: Yale University Press, 1959); Andre Gunder Frank, "The Development of Underdevelopment," *Monthly Review* (September 1966): 11–23; and the *CEPAL Review,* the publication of the UN Economic Commission for Latin America and the Caribbean, during this period.

15. This is covered in the more recent work by John Rapley, *Understanding Development: Theory and Practice in the Third World* (Boulder, Colo.: Lynne Reinner, 2002), pp. 30–33.

16. For the classics on this, see Nyerere's writings and speeches, including Julius Nyerere, *Freedom and Development* (Dar-es-Salaam: Government Printer, 1973). For an interesting analysis (which was not yet written when we were graduate students), see Joel D. Barkan, "Divergence and Convergence in Kenya and Tanzania: Pressures for Reform," in Joel D. Barkan, ed., *Beyond Capitalism vs. Socialism in Kenya & Tanzania* (Boulder, Colo.: Lynne Reinner, 1994).

17. For more detail from a former UNCTAD official, see Nassau Adams, *Worlds Apart: The North-South Divide and the International System* (London: Zed Books, 1993). See also Chandra Hardy, "Toward a Self-Reliant South: Trading Its Way out of a Long Crisis," North-South Institute, 1990.

18. For the New International Economic Order (NIEO) declaration plus its attached "programme of action," see Karl P. Savant and Joachim W. Müller, *The Third World Without Superpowers,* 2d series, vol. 20: *The Collected Documents of the Group of 77* (New York: OCEANA Publications, 1995), pp. 337–354.

19. For more on how ICAs worked, see Nassau Adams's *Worlds Apart,* as well as Belinda Coote, "You Can't Pay the Doctor in Millet: Controlling International Commodity Prices," in *The Trade Trap* (Oxford: Oxfam, 1992).

20. See, for instance, Mark Weisbrot and Dean Baker, "The Relative Impact of Trade Liberalization in Developing Countries," Center for Economic and Policy Research, Washington, D.C., 2002.

21. Naomi Klein has done a detailed analysis of Milton Friedman's impact on Chile and other countries in *The Shock Doctrine: The Rise of Disaster Capitalism* (New York: Metropolitan Books, 2007). See also J. Richard Peet, *Geography of Power: The Making of Global Economic Policy* (London: Zed, 2007).

22. Orlando Letelier, "Economic 'Freedom's' Awful Toll," *The Nation,* August 28, 1976. See also Walden Bello's November 2007 review of Naomi Klein's *The Shock Doctrine* in "Foreign Policy in Focus" (http://www.fpif.org/fpiftxt/4725).

Notes to Chapter 2

An earlier version of this chapter originally appeared as "No More NICs," *Foreign Policy* no. 72 (Fall 1988), www.foreignpolicy.com. Copyright 1988, Carnegie Endowment for International Peace. Authors hold copyright.

1. C. Heatherly and B. Y. Pines, eds., *Mandate for Leadership III: Policy Strate-gies for the 1990s* (Washington, D.C.: Heritage Foundation, 1989), p. 674.

2. Bela Balassa, "The Process of Industrial Development and Alternative Development Strategies," in *International Finance* 141 (Princeton: Princeton University, 1980), pp. 25–26.

3. Interview conducted by Robin Broad with World Bank official (anonymity requested), March 4, 1981.

4. John Williamson, *Lending Policies of the International Monetary Fund,* Policy Analyses in International Economics Series, no. 1 (Washington, D.C.: Institute for International Economics, 1982), p. 22.

5. Argentina, Chile, Colombia, Costa Rica, Cyprus, Dominican Republic, Ecuador, Egypt, Guatemala, Honduras, Indonesia, the Ivory Coast, Jordan, Kenya, Malaysia, Morocco, Pakistan, Paraguay, Peru, the Philippines, Rwanda, Senegal, Sri Lanka, Syria, Thailand, Tunisia, Turkey, Uruguay, Venezuela, and Zambia.

6. The Philippine case study is expanded in Robin Broad, *Unequal Alliance: The World Bank, the International Monetary Fund, and the Philippines,* Studies in International Political Economy series (Stephen Krasner, series editor) (Berkeley: University of California Press, 1988; Manila: Ateneo de Manila University Press, 1988; first paperback printing by University of California Press, 1990).

7. World Bank, *Industrial Development Strategy and Policies in the Philippines,* Report 2513-PH, October 29, 1979, vol. 1, p. 2.

8. World Bank, *Philippines: Staff Appraisal Report on the Industrial Finance Project,* Report 3331-PH (Washington, D.C. April 7, 1981), p. 4.

9. Statistics calculated from IMF, *Annual Report of the Executive Board for the Financial Year Ended April 30, 1981* (Washington, D.C.: IMF, 1981), p. 8, table 1. Other statistics from IMF, *World Economic Outlook: A Survey by the Staff of the IMF,* Occasional Paper 9 (Washington, D.C.: IMF, 1982), p. 31.

10. H. Chenery and D. Keesing, *The Changing Composition of Developing Country Exports,* World Bank Staff Working Paper 314, January 1979, p. 42.

11. See, for example, World Bank, *Report and Recommendation of the President of the International Bank for Reconstruction and Development on a Proposed Structural Adjustment Loan to the Republic of the Philippines,* Report P-2872-PH, August 21, 1980, p. 31; World Bank, *World Development Report 1978,* p. 32; Barend de Vries, *Transition Toward More Rapid and Labor-Intensive Development: The Case of the Philippines,* World Bank Working Paper 424, October 1980, p. 17; World Bank, *Philippines Country Program Paper,* March 26, 1976, p 14.

12. World Bank, *Report and Recommendation of the President of the IBRD on a Proposed Structural Adjustment Loan to the Republic of the Philippines,* Report P-2872-PH (Washington, D.C. August 21, 1980), p. 31.

13. Vice President and Secretary, World Bank, *Summaries of the Discussions at the Meeting of the Executive Directors of the Bank and IDA, September 16, 1980,* SD80–52, November 20, 1980, p. 8.

14. World Bank, Operations Evaluation Department, *Structural Adjustment Lending: A First Review of Experience,* Report No. 6409, September 24, 1987, pp. iv, 83, 85.

15. Note that Robin worked on the Baker plan while at the U.S. Treasury Department. See Robin Broad, "How About a Real Solution to Third World Debt?" *New York Times,* September 28, 1987. Reprinted as: "Now for a Serious Response to Third World Debt," *International Herald Tribune,* September 28, 1987.

16. Saburo Okita, "Pacific Development and Its Implication for the World Economy," in *The Pacific Basin: New Challenges for the United States,* ed. James W. Morley (New York: The Academy of Political Science in conjunction with the East Asian Institute and the Center on Japanese and Business Economy, Columbia University, 1986), p. 30.

Notes to Chapter 3

An earlier version of this chapter, coauthored with Walden Bello, originally appeared as "Development: The Market Is Not Enough," *Foreign Policy* no. 81 (Winter 1990–1991) www.foreignpolicy.com. Copyright 1991, Carnegie Endowment for International Peace. Reproduced with permission.

1. Quoted in Clyde H. Farnsworth, "Conable's World Bank: Finding Fault and Praise," *New York Times,* February 1, 1980.

2. United Nations Children's Fund, *The State of the World's Children 1990* (New York: Oxford University Press, 1990); and Oxfam America, *In a World of Abundance: Why Hunger?* (Boston: Oxfam America, 1990), p. 8.

3. Quoted in Roger Cohen, "Poor Youths in Brazil Get Fatal Kicks Atop Trains," *Asian Wall Street Journal,* November 4–5, 1988, p. 1.

4. The source for information on South Korea and Taiwan in this chapter is: Walden Bello and Stephanie Rosenfeld, *Dragons In Distress: Asia's Miracle Economies in Crisis* (San Francisco: Institute for Food and Development Policy / Food First, 1990).

5. "Most People Here Put Environmental Protection Before Economic Growth," *China News* (Taipei), May 5, 1985.

6. UNCTAD, *Handbook of International Trade and Development Statistics 1984* (New York: UNCTAD, 1984), p. 386.

7. "Capitalism's Coming Costs," *Japan Times,* December 29, 1989.

8. See, for instance, Rensselear W. Lee III, "Issues in Chinese Economic Reform," in *Economic Reform in Three Giants,* eds. Richard E. Feinberg, John Escheverri-Gent, and Friedemann Muller (New Brunswick, N.J.: Transaction Books, 1990), pp. 83–84.

9. See John Williamson, *The Progress of Policy Reform in Latin America,* Policy Analyses in International Economics, no. 28 (Washington, D.C.: Institute for International Economics, January 1990).

10. For the World Bank's role in Costa Rica, see Iona Sebastian and Adelaida Alicbusan, "Sustainable Development: Issues in Adjustment Lending," Divisional Paper No. 1989–6, World Bank, Policy and Research Division, Environment

Department, October 1989. The classic account of deforestation in Costa Rica is Norman Myers's "The Hamburger Connection: How Central America's Forests Became North America's Hamburgers," *Ambio* 10 (1981): 3–8. For an update on Costa Rica, see Richard Sandbrook, Marc Edelman, Patrick Heller, and Judith Teichman, *Social Democracy in the Global Periphery: Origin, Challenges, Prospects* (Cambridge, U.K.: Cambridge University Press, 2007).

11. F. Bourginon, William Branson, and J. de Melo, "Adjustment and Income Distribution: A Counterfactual Analysis," Country Economic Department, Policy Planning and Research, World Bank, May 1989, cover page.

12. George Foy and Herman Daly, "Allocation, Distribution and Scale as Determinants of Environmental Degradation: Case Studies of Haiti, El Salvador and Costa Rica," Environment Department Working Paper No.19, World Bank, September 1989.

13. United Nations Economic Commission for Africa, *African Alternative Framework to Structural Adjustment Programmes for Socio-Economic Recovery and Transformation,* AAF-SAP (Addis Ababa: UN-ECA, 1988), p. 23.

14. For details, see Robin Broad with John Cavanagh, *Plundering Paradise: The Struggle for the Environment in the Philippines* (Berkeley: University of California Press, 1993).

15. Alan Durning, "People Power and Development," *Foreign Policy,* no. 76 (Fall 1989): 66.

16. Claudia Alvarez, "India's Gigantic Harsud Rally Says 'No' to Destructive Projects," *Third World Network Features,* no. 532 (1989).

17. Sandra Steingraber and Judith Hurley, "Brazil's Debt and Deforestation— A Global Warning," in *Food First Action Alert* (San Francisco: Institute for Food and Development Policy, 1990), p. 2.

18. Sheldon Annis and Peter Hakim, *Direct to the Poor: Grassroots Development in Latin America* (Boulder, Colo.: Lynne Rienner, 1988).

19. Fantu Cheru, *The Silent Revolution in Africa* (London: Zed Press, 1989), p. 19. See also David Korten, *Getting to the 21st Century* (West Hartford, Conn.: Kumarian Press, 1990).

20. Congress for People's Agrarian Reform, "Popular Grassroots Initiatives: Towards Genuine Agrarian Reform: A Descriptive Report," unpublished report, Manila, June 1989.

21. See the work of Richard Franke and Barbara Chasin, including "Development Without Growth: The Kerala Experiment," *Technology Review* (April 1990): 43–50. For an update on Kerala, see Richard Sandbrook, Marc Edelman, Patrick Heller, and Judith Teichman, *Social Democracy in the Global Periphery: Origin, Challenges, Prospects* (Cambridge, U.K.: Cambridge University Press, 2007).

22. Atul Kohli, "Democracy and Development," in *Development Strategies Reconsidered,* eds. John P. Lewis and Valeriana Kallab (New Brunswick, N.J.: Transaction Books, 1986), pp. 3–25.

23. On this, see Charles William Maynes, "America Without the Cold War," *Foreign Policy,* no. 78 (Spring 1990): 3–25.

Notes to Chapter 4

An earlier version of this chapter originally appeared as "Beyond the Myths of Rio: A New American Agenda for the Environment," *World Policy Journal* 10 (Spring 1993). Authors hold copyright.

1. See "NAFTA Pork: Free Lunch for Corporations and Congress," *CovertAction* (Winter 1993–1994): 25, which is based on information compiled by Public Citizen and Citizens Trade Campaign.

2. For more on this case and others, as well as an expanded analysis based on Philippine fieldwork funded by the John D. and Catherine T. MacArthur Foundation, see our *Plundering Paradise: The Struggle for the Environment in the Philippines* (Berkeley: University of California Press, 1993).

3. Vandana Shiva, "Real Versus Pseudo Greens in the New Politics," *Third World Network Features,* no. 827/91 (1991): 1.

4. Gene Grossman, "Poor Regions, Environmental Law," *New York Times,* March 1, 1992. See Gene Grossman and Alan Krueger, "Environmental Impacts of a North American Free Trade Agreement," Discussion Papers in Economics, No. 158 (Princeton: Woodrow Wilson School of Public and International Affairs, November 1991).

5. Summers is quoted in *IMF Survey,* vol. 21, no. 16 (August 3, 1992): 245. Summers subsequently was promoted to U.S. Treasury secretary, and then went on to become president of Harvard University from 2001 to 2006.

6. Quoted in William Greider, "How We Export Jobs and Disease," *Rolling Stone,* September 3, 1992, p. 32.

7. Editorial, "Limping Home from Rio," *Washington Post,* June 14, 1992.

8. See David Korten, "Sustainable Development: A Review Essay," *World Policy Journal,* vol. 9, no. 1 (Winter 1991–1992): 157–190.

9. See Pat Aufderheide and Bruce Rich, "Environmental Reform and the Multilateral Development Banks," *World Policy Journal,* vol. 5, no. 2 (Spring 1988): 301–321; and Bruce Rich, *Mortgaging the Earth: The World Bank, Environmental Impoverishment, and the Crisis of Development* (Boston: Beacon Press, 1994). See also the publications of the Bank Information Center, the International Rivers Network, and the Development GAP.

10. Mexican Action Network on Free Trade, Alliance for Responsible Trade, and Citizens Trade Campaign with Action Canada Network, "A Just and Sustainable Trade and Development Initiative for North America," November 28, 1993. (This document is excerpted in Broad, *Global Backlash,* pp. 129–134.) See also George E. Brown, Jr., J. William Goold, and John Cavanagh, "Making Trade Fair," *World Policy Journal* vol. 9, no. 2 (Spring 1992): 309–327; and Jorge Castaneda and Carlos Heredia, "Another NAFTA: What a Good Agreement Should Offer," *World Policy Journal* (Winter 1992–1993): 673–685.

11. Al Gore, *Earth in the Balance* (Boston: Houghton Mifflin, 1992), p. 343.

12. See Frances F. Korten, "Questioning the Call for Environmental Loans:

A Critical Examination of Forestry Lending in the Philippines," *World Development,* vol. 22, no. 7 (July 1994): 971–981.

13. The Development GAP, Bread for the World, the Sierra Club, et al., "The Development Cooperation Act of 1990: A Proposal for U.S. Support of Equitable and Sustainable Development." See also Stephen Hellinger, Douglas Hellinger, and Fred O'Regan, *Aid for Just Development: Report on the Future of Foreign Assistance* (Boulder, Colo.: Lynne Reinner, 1988).

Notes to Chapter 5

An earlier version of this chapter originally appeared as "Don't Neglect the Impoverished South," *Foreign Policy* no. 101 (Winter 1995–1996), www.foreignpolicy.com. Copyright 1996, Carnegie Endowment for International Peace. Reprinted with permission.

1. See, for instance, Jeffrey Garten, U.S. Under-Secretary of Commerce for International Trade, "The Big Emerging Markets: Changing American Interests in the Global Economy," Remarks before the Foreign Policy Association, New York, January 20, 1994.

2. Quoted in *Earth Times,* November 15, 1994, p. 11.

3. John Stremlau, "Clinton's Dollar Diplomacy," *Foreign Policy* no. 97 (Winter 1994–1995): 19.

4. See, for example, World Bank, *World Atlas 1995* (Washington, D.C.: World Bank, 1995).

5. Calculated from World Bank, *World Bank Tables 1992–93: External Finance for Developing Countries,* vol. 1: *Analysis and Summary* (Washington, D.C.: World Bank, December 1992), p. 160.

6. World Bank, *World Development Report 1993* (New York: Oxford University Press, 1993), p. 239.

7. UNDP, *Human Development Report 1994* (New York: Oxford University Press, 1994), p. 143.

8. Keith Griffin and Terry McKinley, "A Global Balance Sheet," draft paper for UNDP, 1994.

9. World Bank, *World Debt Tables, 1994–95,* vol. 1 (Washington, D.C., 1994), table 2.1, p. 25.

10. *World Debt Tables, 1992–93,* pp. 16, 17.

11. Calculated by authors from UN, *World Economic and Social Survey 1994,* (New York, 1994), p. 21.

12. *World Economic and Social Survey 1994,* p. 22.

13. *World Debt Tables, 1994-95,* p. 11.

14. *Washington Post,* December 31, 1994, p. A28.

15. *World Economic and Social Survey 1994,* p. 278. This is calculated through

a dollar index deflated by unit values of manufactured exports of Northern countries.

16. *World Economic and Social Survey 1994,* p. 96.

17. Richard J. Barnet and John Cavanagh, *Global Dreams: Imperial Corporations and the New World Order* (New York: Simon & Schuster, 1994).

18. "For Richer, For Poorer," *The Economist,* November 5, 1994, p. 19 (first quote) and p. 20 (second quote).

19. UNDP, *Human Development Report 1994,* p. 35.

20. Calculated by the authors from "The Billionaires," *Forbes,* July 18, 1994; "The World's Billionaires," *Forbes,* October 5, 1987; "The Forbes 400," *Forbes,* October 26, 1987; UNDP, p. 63; and World Bank, *World Development Report 1993,* pp. 239, 243.

21. Calculated by the authors from 2007 data from *Forbes* magazine and the United Nations University's World Institute for Development Economics Research.

22. See Jeremy Brecher and Tim Costello, *Global Village or Global Pillage: Economic Reconstruction from the Bottom Up* (Boston: South End Press, 1994).

23. UNDP, p. 164; *World Development Report 1993,* pp. 238, 243; and *Forbes,* July 18, 1994.

24. *The Economist,* May 6, 1995, p. 18.

Notes to Chapter 6

An earlier version of this chapter originally appeared as "The Death of the Washington Consensus?" *World Policy Journal* vol. 16, no. 3 (Fall 1999). Authors hold the copyright.

1. On this, see the work of Kate Bronfenbrenner at Cornell, such as "Uneasy Terrain: The Impact of Capital Mobility on Workers, Wages and Union Organizing," Report to the U.S. Trade Deficit Review Commission, September 6, 2000, http://www.ustdrc.gov.

2. Jackie Calmes, "Despite Buoyant Economic Times, Americans Don't Buy Free Trade," *Wall Street Journal,* December 10, 1998.

3. M. Drohan, "How the Net Killed the MAI," *Globe and Mail,* April 30, 1998.

4. International Confederation of Free Trade Unions, ICFTU Online, January 21, 1999.

5. Jeffrey Sachs, "The IMF and the Asian Flu," *American Prospect,* March–April 1998, p. 17.

6. This group became the dominant voice in the Meltzer Commission. See A. Meltzer et al., *Report of the International Financial Institution Advisory Commission* (Washington, D.C.: US Government Printing Office, 2000).

7. See Michael Shari, "Up In Smoke," *Business Week,* June 1, 1998, p. 66.

8. Wolfensohn's tenure was marked by backsliding on a number of these issues, including withdrawing from the structural adjustment loan (SAL) review

exercise. See *Structural Adjustment—The SAPRI Report: The Policy Roots of Economic Crisis, Poverty and Inequality* (New York: Zed Books, 2004), and www.saprin.org. For a positive take on the World Bank, see Sebastian Mallaby, *The World's Banker: A Story of Failed States, Financial Crises, and the Wealth and Poverty of Nations* (New York: Penguin, 2004). For a more critical assessment (that meshes more with the current authors' views), see the work of the Bank Information Center, Fifty Years Is Enough Network, Bretton Woods Project (in the United Kingdom), Focus on the Global South (with main headquarters in Bangkok), Third World Network (Malaysia headquarters), and the collective "IFI-watchers" site: www.ifiwatch. org. See Dana Clark, Jonathan Fox, and Kay Treakle, *Demanding Accountability: Civil-Society Claims and the World Bank Inspection Panel* (Lanham, Md.: Rowman & Littlefield, 2003); see the edition of this book published in India (Rainbow Publishers, 2003) for Smitu Kothari's preface.

9. Ngaire Woods, *The Globalizers: The IMF, the World Bank and Their Borrowers* (Ithaca: Cornell University Press, 2006), pp. 162–167. By September 2006, twenty countries had made it to the "completion point" under HIPC that "won" them some debt relief. See United Nations, *World Economic Situation and Prospects 2007* (New York: United Nations, 2007), p. 71.

10. Jagdish Bhagwati, "The Capital Myth: The Difference Between Trade in Widgets and Dollars," *Foreign Affairs,* vol. 77 (May–June 1998): 7.

11. Bhagwati, "Capital Myth," p. 12.

12. Joseph Stiglitz, "More Instruments and Broader Goals: Moving toward the Post-Washington Consensus," 1998 World Institute for Development Economics Research annual lecture, Helsinki, Finland, January 7, 1998. Note, however, that Stiglitz places blame more on the IMF and U.S. Treasury than on the World Bank.

13. Patrick Bond's account from southern Africa suggests that Stiglitz's criticisms were more subdued in the field. See Patrick Bond, *Elite Transition: From Apartheid to Neoliberalism in South Africa* 2d ed. (London: Zed, 2005), pp. 339–344.

14. See Robert Hunter Wade, "What Strategies Are Viable for Developing Countries Today? The World Trade Organization and the Shrinking of 'Development Space,'" *Review of International Political Economy* vol. 10, no. 4 (November 2003): 621–644. On the WTO, see also the work of: Timothy Wise and Kevin Gallagher at the Global Development and Environment Institute at Tufts University (http://ase.tufts.edu/gdae); Eileen Kwa (Focus on the Global South); Martin Khor (Third World Network/ SUNS); and Sandra Polaski (Carnegie Endowment for International Peace, www.CarnegieEndowment.org).

15. See Friends of the Earth, International Forum on Globalization, and Third World Network, "Call to Action: A Citizens Agenda for Reform of the Global Economic System," Washington, D.C., December 10, 1998; and Robert Blecker, *Taming Global Finance: A Better Architecture for Growth and Equity* (Washington, D.C.: Economic Policy Institute, 1999). For papers from the March 1999 Focus on the Global South conference in Bangkok, see Walden Bello, Nicola Bullard, and Kamal Malhotra, eds., *Global Finance: New Thinking on Regulating Speculative Capital Markets* (London: Zed Press, 2000).

Notes to Chapter 7

An earlier version of this chapter originally appeared as "The Hijacking of the Development Debate: How Friedman and Sachs Got It Wrong," *World Policy Journal* vol. 23, no. 2. Copyright World Policy Journal (via MIT Press). Reproduced with permission.

1. Thomas L. Friedman, *The World Is Flat: A Brief History of the Twenty-First Century* (New York: Farrar, Strauss and Giroux, 2005); Jeffrey D. Sachs, *The End of Poverty: Economic Possibilities for Our Time* (New York: Penguin Books, 2005).

2. Belén Balanyá, Brid Brennan, Olivier Hoedeman, Satoko Kishimoto, and Philipp Terhorst, eds., *Reclaiming Public Water: Achievements, Struggles and Visions from Around the World* (Amsterdam: Transnational Institute and Corporate Europe Observatory, January 2005).

3. Jeffrey D. Sachs, "The End of Poverty," *Time*, March 14, 2002.

4. Friedman, *World Is Flat*, p. 330. Unless otherwise noted, Friedman citations refer to this book.

5. The International Forum on Globalization, created in 1994, has brought together leading researchers and activists from North and South to understand the many ramifications of economic globalization and to seek alternatives. See www.ifg.org.

6. Jan Vandemoortele, "Are We Really Reducing Global Poverty?" United Nations Development Program, July 2002, pp. 2–3. On poverty, aid, trade, and climate, see also the policy papers of: ActionAid (www.actionaid.org), Oxfam America (www.oxfamamerica.org), Oxfam International (www.oxfam.org), and the Center for Global Development (www.cgdev.org).

7. Vandemoortele, p. 7.

8. Sachs, *End of Poverty*, pp. 2, 24, 244. Sachs wants to clean up this "clinical poverty" through "clinical economics," building on the image of "modern medicine, a profession of rigor, insight and practicality" (p. 74). Unless otherwise noted, Sachs citations refer to this book.

9. Friedman, p. 382.

10. Friedman, p. 97.

11. Friedman, pp. 9–11, 185.

12. Friedman, p. 316. Friedman has a tendency to resort to such hyperbole. Indeed, in this case, he qualifies "everyone" only by adding that he is not talking about "Chileans" or "energetic immigrants."

13. Friedman, p. 383.

14. Sachs, p. 31. Emphasis in the original.

15. Sachs, p. 18.

16. "Middle class is a state of mind, not a state of income" (Friedman, p. 375).

17. Friedman, pp. 373–374.

18. Vandana Shiva, "How to End Poverty: Making Poverty History and the History of Poverty," unpublished paper, March 28, 2005.

19. See Walter Rodney, *How Europe Underdeveloped Africa,* rev. ed. (Washington, D.C.: Howard University Press, 1982).

20. See Branko Milanovic's *Worlds Apart: Measuring International and Global Inequality* (Princeton: Princeton University Press, 2005); see also United Nations Conference on Trade and Development, *Trade and Development Report, 1997* (Geneva, 1997); United Nations Development Program, *Human Development Report, 1999* (New York, 1999).

21. Vandemoortele, "Are We Really Reducing Global Poverty?" pp. 11–13.

22. W. W. Rostow, *The Stages of Economic Growth: A Non-Communist Manifesto,* 2d ed. (Cambridge: Cambridge University Press, 1971), chapters 2, 3. Sachs indeed uses the word "take-off" (for example, see p. 31) and "preconditions" (for example, see p. 3).

23. William Easterly, "Tone Deaf on Africa," *New York Times,* July 3, 2005. See Easterly's *The White Man's Burden: Why the West's Efforts to Aid the Rest Have Done So Much Ill and So Little Good* (New York: Penguin, 2006).

24. Betsy Hartmann and James Boyce, *Needless Hunger: Voices from a Bangladesh Village* (San Francisco: Institute for Food and Development Policy, 1979); and *A Quiet Violence: View from a Bangladesh Village* (San Francisco: Institute for Food and Development Policy, 1983).

25. Ben Wisner, quoted in Lloyd Timberlake, *Africa in Crisis: The Causes, the Cures of Environmental Bankruptcy* (London: Earthscan, 1986), p. 219.

26. See, for example, the work of Caleb Rossiter, esp. "Poverty in a Time of Empire: Why Foreign Aid Can't 'Make Poverty History,'" unpublished paper, 2006, available at www.calebrossiter.com.

27. Sarah Anderson and the Global Economic Justice Task Force of the Institute for Policy Studies, "Debt Boomerang 2006: How Americans Would Benefit from Cancellation of Impoverished Country Debts," Institute for Policy Studies, March 2006, http://ips-dc.org/boomerang/DB2006.pdf. See also Susan George, *A Fate Worse Than Debt: A Radical New Analysis of the Third World Debt Crisis* (London: Penguin Books, 1988).

28. Sachs, pp. 3, 356–357.

29. Friedman, p. 248.

30. Friedman, p. 314.

31. Friedman, p. 315.

32. Vandemoortele, "Are We Really Reducing Global Poverty?" pp. 2–3.

33. From UNCTAD meeting on "Commodities and Development," February 7, 2006, as discussed in Martin Khor, "UNCTAD Commission Debates the Crisis in Commodities," TWN (Third World Network) Info Service on WTO and Trade Issues, February 13, 2006.

34. "The Economics of Failure: The Real Cost of 'Free' Trade for Poor Countries," Christian Aid briefing paper (London, June 2005), p. 1.

35. This is research by World Bank economists David Dollar and Art Kraay. For a critique of Dollar's and Kraay's work and the "paradigm maintenance" role of

World Bank research, see Robin Broad, "Research, Knowledge & The Art of 'Paradigm Maintenance': The World Bank's Development Economics Vice-Presidency (DEC)," *Review of International Political Economy* vol. 13, no. 3 (August 2006).

36. Mark Weisbrot, "The Scorecard on Development: 25 Years of Diminished Progress," Center for Economic and Policy Research, unpublished paper, September 2005; Dani Rodrik, *The Global Governance of Trade As If Development Really Mattered* (New York: United Nations Development Program, 2001), p. 22; and Dani Rodrik, *One Economics, Many Recipes: Globalization, Institutions, and Economic Growth* (Princeton: Princeton University Press, 2008). See also Ravi Kanbur, "Economic Policy, Distribution, and Poverty: The Nature of Disagreements," *World Development,* vol. 29, no. 6 (2001): 1083–1094, and "Extract from Growth and Trade: The Last Redoubt?" available at www.cornell. edu/poverty/kanbur; and Robert Hunter Wade, "Is Globalization Reducing Poverty and Inequality?" *World Development,* vol. 32, no. 4 (2004).

37. See Robert Hunter Wade, "What Strategies Are Viable for Developing Countries Today? The World Trade Organization and the Shrinking of 'Development Space,'" *Review of International Political Economy,* vol. 10 (November 2003): 621–644.

38. Friedman, p. 314.

39. See the special issue of *WorldWatch Magazine* on "Peak Oil," January–February 2006; Richard Heinberg, *The Party's Over: Oil, War and the Fate of Industrial Societies* (Gabriola Island, British Colombia: New Society Publishers, 2003); and Maude Barlow and Tony Clarke, *Blue Gold: The Fight to Stop the Corporate Threat to the World's Water* (New York: New Press, 2002).

40. Friedman, p. 227.

41. Friedman, p. 237; see also p. 226.

Notes to Chapter 8

1. Steven R. Weissman, "3 Global Financial Institutions' Roles Questioned," *New York Times,* May 23, 2007.

2. See Bhumika Muchhala, ed., *Ten Years After: Revisiting the Asian Financial Crisis* (Woodrow Wilson International Center for Scholars Asia Program, October 2007).

3. EURODAD, "Untying the Knots: How the World Bank Is Failing to Deliver Real Changes on Conditionality," European Network on Debt and Development Report, www.eurodad.org, 2007, p. 3. A later EURODAD report concluded that the IMF was likewise failing to reduce the number of onerous conditions attached to its loans. See Nuria Molina and Javier Pereira, "Critical Conditions: The IMF Maintains its Grip on Low-Income Governments," EURODAD, April 2008.

4. Robin Broad, "Research, Knowledge & the Art of 'Paradigm Maintenance': The World Bank's Development Economics Vice-Presidency (DEC),"

Review of International Political Economy vol. 13, no. 3 (August 2006). Some months after the publication of Robin's article, the *Financial Times* reported on an extensive external review of DEC headed by (among others) Princeton economist Angus Deaton and former head of research at the IMF Ken Rogoff. The review reached conclusions that were shockingly similar to Robin's. See Eoin Callan, "World Bank 'Uses Doubtful Evidence to Push Policies,'" *Financial Times,* December 22, 2006. The "audit" report is "An Evaluation of World Bank Research, 1998–2005," September 24, 2006, available on the World Bank website under DEC.

5. Mark Weisbrot, "Latin America: The End of an Era," *International Journal of Health Services* vol. 36, no. 4, 2006. See other work of the Center for Economic and Policy Research (www.cepr.org). The quotation is from David J. Lynch, "Argentina's Snub of Conventional Wisdom Pays Off," *USA Today,* November 7, 2007.

6. "The IMF Faces Financial Troubles of Its Own," *The Economist,* February 3, 2007, U.S. edition.

7. See, among others, Bob Davis, "Zoellick Charts Inclusive Course at World Bank," *Wall Street Journal,* October 9, 2007. On World Bank climate lending, see Janet Redman, "World Bank: Climate Profiteer," Institute for Policy Studies, April 2008.

8. Soren Ambrose and Bhumika Muchhala, "Changing of the Guard at the IMF," Foreign Policy in Focus, October 31, 2007 (www.fpif.org); and Bob Davis, "IMF Plans to Cut Jobs, Life Income," *Wall Street Journal,* December 7, 2007, and "Excerpts from the Interview: 'We're Not Really in a Crisis,'" www.onlinewsj.com/articles.

9. Celia Dugger, "Ending Famine, Simply by Ignoring the Experts," *New York Times,* December 2, 2007.

10. The quotation is from Timothy A. Wise and Kevin P. Gallagher, "Doha Round and Developing Countries: Will the Doha Deal Do More Harm Than Good?" RIS Policy Briefs, no. 22, Research and Information System for Developing Countries, April 2006, www.ris.org.in. Wise and Gallagher are at Tuft's Global Development and Environment Institute. See also Sandra Polaski, "The Future of the WTO," Carnegie Endowment for International Peace, Policy Outlook, September 2006; and Robert H. Wade, "The Doha Talks Must Fail for the Sake of the World's Poor," *The Guardian,* July 3, 2006.

11. Mark Weisbrot, "President Bush's Trip to Latin America Is All About Denial," Center for Economic and Policy Research, March 2007.

12. Jacques Leslie, "The Last Empire," *Mother Jones,* January/February 2008, p. 30; and Walden Bello, "The Environmental Movement in the South: Pivotal Actor in the Fight Against Global Warming," Annual Mellon-Sawyer Public Lecture, Duke University, Durham, North Carolina, October 2, 2007.

13. See James Fallows, "China Makes, the World Takes," *The Atlantic,* July/August 2007, p. 50.

14. Article by Patricia Cohen in the *New York Times,* July 11, 2007, A17.

15. See David Korten, *The Great Turning: From Empire to Earth Community*

(San Francisco: Berrett-Koehler, 2006); Frances Moore Lappe and Anna Lappe, *Hope's Edge: The Next Diet for a Small Planet* (New York: Putnam, 2002); and Paul J. Nelson and Ellen Dorsey, *New Rights Advocacy: Changing Strategies of Development and Human Rights NGOs* (Washington, D.C.: Georgetown Univrsity Press, 2008).

16. John Cavanagh and Jerry Mander, eds., *Alternatives to Economic Globalization: A Better World Is Possible,* second ed. (San Francisco: Berrett-Koehler, 2004). "Subsidiarity" refers to encouraging as much economic activity as possible to remain first local, then regional, then national, turning to the global economy only for goods and services not available at these other levels.

17. Interview with Olivera in *Yes! Magazine,* Summer 2007, p. 26.

18. Eric Holt-Gimenez, *Campesino a Campesino: Voices from Latin America's Farmer to Farmer Movement* (Oakland, Calif.: Food First Books, 2006).

19. Tina Hodges, "Bolivia's Gas Nationalization: Opportunity and Challenges (2)," Andean Information Network, December 4, 2007, http://ain-bolivia.org.

20. Note that Bello works part of the year in Thailand. Walden Bello, "All Fall Down: Ten Years After the Asian Financial Crisis," Foreign Policy in Focus, July 29, 2007.

21. UN Development Program, *Thailand Human Development Report 2007: Sufficiency Economy and Human Development* (Bangkok: UNDP, 2007).

22. "Jubilee South/Americas to Hold Activities in Quito in Support of the Recently Launched Official Debt Audit," Jubileo Sur, August 10, 2007, p. 1, www.jubileosuramerica.blogspot.com.

23. Sarah Anderson, "The Equity Factor & Free Trade," *World Policy Journal* (2003): 45–51.

24. David Harris and Diego Azzi, "ALBA: Venezuela's Answer to 'Free Trade,'" Focus on the Global South and the Hemispheric Social Alliance, October 2006. See also "8 Hotspots of Progress," *Yes! Magazine,* Summer 2007: 21; also from that issue of *Yes! Magazine,* see the articles by Nadia Martinez, "Democracy Rising," pp. 18–19, and Jubenal Quispe, "Bolivia's Indigenous Uprising," p. 25.

25. Vince McElhinny, "Bank of the South: A Look into the New Bank of the South, Due to Launch in December 2007," Bank Information Center Info Brief, November 2007, www.bicusa.org; and Lourdes Heredia, "Why South America Wants a New Bank," BBC News, December 10, 2007.

26. Yung Chul Park and Yunjong Wang, "The Chiang Mai Initiative and Beyond," *The World Economy* (January 2005) vol. 28, no. 1: 91–101; and Vince McElhinney, "Bank of the South," Bank Information Center Info Brief, November 2007, www.bicusa.org, p. 3.

27. See John Cavanagh and Jerry Mander, eds., *Alternatives to Economic Globalization* and Workshop on International Regulations, *How to Regulate and Control Neo-Liberal Globalization* (Tokyo: Pacific Asia Resource Center, 2007); note especially Walden Bello's synthesis chapter, pp. 17–38.

28. See www.jubileeusa.org, and www.jubileesouth.org.

29. On "global climate justice," see Paul Baer and Tom Athanasiou, "A Brief

Adequacy and Equity-Based Evaluation of Some Prominent Climate Policy Frameworks and Proposals," Heinrich Boell Foundation, Global Issue Paper no. 30, 2007; and "A Call for Climate Talks to Accelerate Global Economic and Energy Transitions, What Bali Must Achieve," signed by 138 citizen leaders, released in Bali on December 10, 2007, at www.ips-dc.org. On water, see Maude Barlow, "A UN Convention on the Right to Water: An Idea Whose Time Has Come," www.blueplanetproject.net, 2007.

30. We should also note that we are not the first to suggest such questions. For instance, for a still very relevant and related list of the "right questions," see Lloyd Timberlake, *Africa in Crisis: The Causes, the Cures of Environmental Bankruptcy* (Philadelphia: Earthscan, 1986), pp. 218–219.

31. "For the South Bank Oriented to a Sovereign and Sustainable Development Matrix for the Integration of the Continent in Solidarity," second open letter to the Presidents of Argentina, Bolivia, Brazil, Ecuador, Paraguay, Uruguay, and Venezuela," December 7, 2007, www.cadtm.org/spip.php?article2974.

32. Amy E. Robertson, "Ecuador Invites World to Save Its Forest" [2007], http://news.yahoo.com/s/csm/20070605/wl_csm/ogreenrev.

33. The World Bank launched such a "Forest Carbon Partnership Facility" at the UN Framework Convention on Climate Change, COP-13, in Bali, Indonesia, in December 2007.

Acknowledgments

This book was written over a two-decade period during which literally hundreds of individuals opened up their homes, their lives, their minds, and their hearts to the two of us, and to each of them we extend our thanks.

Walden Bello, who coauthored Chapter 3, is one of the most creative "public scholars" we know; we are indebted to him for his three decades of friendship and prescient insights on development and globalization. Sarah Anderson, Marc Raskin, the late Dick Barnet, and the rest of John's colleagues at the Institute for Policy Studies have provided nurture of many kinds for a quarter-century. So too have Robin's colleagues and students in the International Development Program at American University's School of International Service created an intellectual home for nearly two decades. In addition, Jerry Mander and the staff and board of the International Forum on Globalization have been constant companions in the journey to redefine development.

The late Bill Maynes at *Foreign Policy*, and Linda Wrigley and the late James Chace at *World Policy*, were editors whose love for their craft improved our writing skills.

The John D. and Catherine T. MacArthur Foundation provided us both with a year (1988–1989) of rich interaction with citizen organizations in the Philippines. For Robin, this built on earlier transformative years there, thanks to the Henry Luce Foundation (1977–1978) and Princeton University (1980–1981). Other foundations that generously supported forays (for one or both of us) into the globalization and development debates are: the CS Fund, the CS Mott Foundation, the Ford Foundation, the

Foundation for Deep Ecology, the HKH Foundation, the Max and Anna Levinson Foundation, the Moriah Fund, the Panta Rhea Foundation, the Rockefeller Brothers Fund, the Samuel Rubin Foundation, the Solidago Foundation, the Town Creek Foundation, and the Wallace Global Fund. Sarah Anderson, Soren Ambrose, Adam Hochschild, Neil Watkins, and Walden Bello somehow found time to offer insightful comments on part or all of the manuscript. Elsa Arismendi, Meara Dietrick (who also read and copyedited the whole manuscript), Doug Kandt, and Sean Morgan provided skilled research assistance.

Marilen Abesamis, Corinne Canlas, Frederick F. Clairmonte, Lisa Dacanay, Richard Falk, Chip Fay, Jonny Fox, Barry Gills, Thea Lee, Smitu Kothari, Fe Mangahas, Roger Mangahas, Butch Montes, Lidy Nacpil, Joel Rocamora, Billy J. de la Rosa, Nikki de la Rosa, Nonette Royo, Vim Santos, Isagani Serrano, Helen Shapiro, Mark Simon, and Hanneke van Eldik Thieme have gifted us with so much kindness and so many ideas that we will never be able to thank them adequately.

Vice President and Executive Editor Jennifer Knerr (whom we followed to Paradigm Publishers) has an uncanny ability to comprehend our book almost better than we do. Her vision, and that of Series Editor Mark Boyer, allowed this book to take its intellectual form. We thank others at Paradigm, including Cover Design Manager Sharon Daugherty, Publishing Associate in College Marketing and Acquisitions Jessica Priest, and Senior Production Editor Carol Smith, who helped produce this book under a expedited schedule.

Finally, we thank our families and especially our now eleven-year-old son Jesse Broad-Cavanagh. Jesse accompanied us on two research trips to Asia and one to Central America and, by and large, put up with our writing as well as our dinner-table conversation. Jesse also helped keep us focused on the key questions—for instance, when as a boy of six, he spent time with children on the streets of Manila and later turned to us and queried, "Why are some children poor and others not?"

Robin Broad and John Cavanagh,
June 2008
Takoma Park, Maryland

Index

Abraham, 1–2, 107

Acheson, Dean, 6

AFL-CIO, 77

Africa, 4, 98; 1960/1970s socialism of, 11; in 1990s, 29, 118n13; poverty in, 83, 86–87, 88; U.S. and, 54

Agency for International Development, 63

Age of Debate (1960–1980), 10

aid: in 21st century, 81; to citizen organizations, 51–52, 63; Clinton administration and, 49, 50; environmental degradation and, 48–49, 51; environmental myths about, 44, 48–49; as grants, 51; as loans, 50–51; poverty and, 86–87; redefining, 50; Sachs, Jeffrey, on, 86, 87, 89; trade and, 87–88; U.S. and, 63. *See also* investments

Alliance of the Peoples of the Forest, 35

alter-globalization: in 1990s, 27–28, 68; in 21st century, 80, 81; 21st century mass citizen gatherings, 80; alternatives in action and, 99–104; citizen organizations and, 100; Consensus *vs.*, 4, 8; developing countries and, 91; development redefinition, 99; environmental sustainability and, 103–104; Friedman, Thomas, and, 88, 89; goals of, 99; HIPC and, 77; history

of, 9–10, 14, 41, 91; Latin America and, 80, 101, 105–106; movement constituents of, 89; movement of, 4, 110n8; present and future of, 92; present day, 99; questions about, 9–10; Sachs, Jeffrey, and, 88, 89; social movements and, 100; terminology of, 110n8; Wal-Mart economy and, 88; Washington Consensus and, 80, 89, 91. *See also* citizen backlash; citizen initiatives; globalization alternatives

Alternatives to Economic Globalization (Cavanagh and Mander), 99, 123n16

Amazon, 35, 101

Andean nations, 11

Annis, Sheldon, 36

Argentina, 96, 100; IMF and, 93

Asia, 4; in 1990s, 29; U.S. and, 54

Asian financial crisis (1997). *See* East Asian Crisis (1997)

Asian Miracles, 14

Asian NICs, 18–19, 26; 1980s lost decade and, 30

Australia, 52

authoritarian governments: democracy and, 39; economic growth and, 39; industrialization and, 39; of South Korea, 39; sustainable development and, 39; of Taiwan, 39

Baker, James, 24
Balassa, Bela, 15
Banco del Sur, 105, 106
Bangladesh, 87
Bank Information Center, 118n8, 123n25, 123n26
Barlow, Maude, 121n39, 124n29
Barnet, Richard, 59
Battle of Seattle, 81
Bello, Walden, 76, 101, 111n22
Bentsen, Lloyd, 44
Berlin Wall, 1989 fall of, 28
Bhagwati, Jagdish, 71, 72, 74
Blair, Tony, 73
Bolivia, 94, 96, 100, 101
Bond, Patrick, 118n13
Bono, 81, 82
Bosnia, 54
bottom 45 percent, 63–64
Boyce, James, 86
Brazil, 15, 35, 36, 45, 96, 99, 100, 101; neoliberalism and, 98
Bretton Woods Project, 118n8
Bukidnon, 1
Bush, George H. W., 43; free trade and, 44, 49–50; NAFTA and, 49–50
Bush, George W., 41; free trade and, 79, 82; September 11, 2001, and, 82, 98
Bush, George W., administration: Friedman, Thomas, and, 82; neoconservatives of, 93; Sachs, Jeffrey, and, 82; terrorism and, 98; Wolfowitz and, 93; World Bank and, 93, 94

Camdessus, Michel, 71, 74
Canada, 43, 52
capitalism, vs. communism, 40
capitalist economies: Japan and, 31; socialist economies vs., 31
Caribbean, 4, 11, 18, 56
Cato Institute, 72
Center for Economic and Policy Research, 88
Central America, 11
Chavez, Hugo, 81, 96
Chenery, Hollis, 18
Cheru, Fantu, 36
Chiang Mai Initiative, 103

Chicago-boys, 12
Chile, 56, 96; free market and, 12, 13
China, 18, 32, 92; economic growth of, 26, 96; environmental crises in, 96–97; environmental degradation and, 62; poverty in, 83, 88; regulation in, 97
Christian Aid, 88
Citibank, 59
citizen backlash: governmental opposition to neoliberalism and, 96; to NAFTA, 43. See also alter-globalization
citizen initiatives, 39–40; in 1990s, 35–40; development failures and, 35–40; environmental activism and, 35, 41; environmental sustainability and, 36; equity and, 35, 36; human needs and, 36; human rights and, 36; in Latin America, 36; political participation and, 35, 36; sustainable development and, 38. See also alter-globalization
citizen movements, 39–40
citizen organizations, 36; 1990's financial crisis and, 77, 78; aid to, 51–52, 63; alter-globalization and, 100; Clinton administration and, 52; countrywide associations and, 36; in India, 38; neoliberalism and, 81; of Philippines, 36–37; political participation and, 37; sustainable development and, 36, 38–39; WTO and, 76
Clinton administration: aid and, 49, 50; citizen organizations and, 52; developing countries debt burden and, 51; environmental sustainability and, 49; flawed policy assumptions of, 56–57; foreign policy of, 54–55; free market and, 5, 55, 59; globalization and, 59; NAFTA and, 42, 43, 49, 50, 55, 56; neoliberalism and, 42; NICs and, 53; North-South gap and, 62; Republican Congress and, 55, 56; the South, 55, 56; Third World and, 54–55; Third World images of, 54–55, 56; Washington Consensus and, 53; WTO and, 56. See also the North; the South; United States
Clinton, Bill, 42, 43, 49, 50
Coca-Cola, 23

Cold War, 54; development after, 40
command economics, 31; Eastern Europe
  socialism and, 30, 31, 32; market
  mechanisms *vs.*, 32; of South Korea,
  31–32
communism *vs.* capitalism, 40
computer revolution, 23
Conable, Barber, 28–29
Consensus. *See* Washington Consensus
corporations: environmental degradation
  and, 49; environmental standards and, 65
Council of Foreign Relations, 7
countrywide associations, 36
Cuba, 54

debt burden, of developing countries, 50;
  canceling of, 63, 77, 87, 103; Clinton
  administration and, 51; IMF and,
  63, 77; World Bank and, 63. *See also*
  developing countries
debt crisis, Third World, 9; causes of,
  23–24; IMF and, 15, 24; North-South
  gap and, 57–58; poor nations and, 14,
  15, 57; Third World and, 23; U.S. and,
  24; World Bank and, 15, 23, 24
democracy: authoritarian governments
  and, 39; economic growth and, 39;
  equity and, 39; sustainable development
  and, 39. *See also* political participation
deregulation, 81; in Washington Consensus economic-reform areas, 109n3
developing countries: alter-globalization
  and, 91; debt burden of, 50–51;
  economic pragmatism and, 38; exports
  and, 16; IMF and, 63, 73, 77; loans
  and, 50–51; NICs and, 32; structural
  adjustment and, 32; UNCTAD
  and, 16; U.S. and, 53; Washington
  Consensus and, 33, 73, 91. *See also*
  debt burden, of developing countries;
  Newly Industrializing Countries; poor
  nations; Third World
development: government role in, 10;
  ladder of, 84, 85; modernization and,
  84–86; questions, 1, 2, 9, 109n1. *See
  also* sustainable development
The Development Cooperation Act
  (1990), 51

development debate: in 1980s, 14; in
  1990s, 28–29, 40, 68, 76; in academia,
  7; academic economists and, 98; Age
  of Debate (1960–1980), 10; history
  of, 5, 7; NAFTA and, 43; post–World
  War II, 10; poverty in, 85; present day,
  96, 98–99; questions for, 104–107; in
  UN, 7
*The Development Dictionary: A Guide to
  Knowledge as Power* (Sachs, W.), 109n1
The Development Group for Alternative
  Policies, 51
development orthodoxy: free market,
  5–6; history of, 5–6
Development Round, 79, 95
Doha Round, 79, 95
Dominican Republic, 54
Durning, Alan, 35

Earth in the Balance (Gore), 42, 50
Earth Summit (1992), 41–42, 48;
  environmental myths at, 43, 47, 49;
  Gore and, 43
East Asia, 1970s rapid exports of, 14
East Asian crisis (1997), 9, 67, 70; IMF
  and, 72, 92, 93
Easterly, William, 86, 120n23
Eastern Europe, 36; socialist command
  economies of, 30, 31, 32
ecological sustainability. *See*
  environmental sustainability
ecology. *See* specific environmental issues
economic activity, environmental
  sustainability and, 47
economic globalization. *See* globalization
economic growth: authoritarian
  governments and, 39; of China, 26,
  96; democracy and, 39; development
  and, 2, 7, 109n1; environmental issues
  and, 2; environmental myths about free
  market, 43–44, 46–48; environmental
  sustainability and, 36; equity *vs.*, 36,
  48; free market and, 2; human needs
  vs., 36; of India, 96; political issues
  and, 2; political participation *vs.*, 36;
  social issues and, 2; tariffs and, 88;
  theory as "fact," 2; trade and, 87, 88;
  Washington Consensus and, 27, 68, 80

economic integration, free trade
    agreements and, 64
economic orthodoxy, global (1980–1985),
    2
economic pragmatism, developing
    countries and, 38
economic reform, Washington Consensus
    and, 3
economics, Keynesian, 10
economies, mature, 37–38
economies of scale, 11
The Economist, 60
economy: government role in, 37. See also
    specific economic topics
Ecuador, 96, 101, 106
Eisenhower, Dwight, 74
The End of Poverty (Sachs, J.), 80, 81
England, 14
enlightened self-interest, 65–66
environmental activism, 28; citizen
    initiatives and, 35, 41; indigenous
    communities and, 35; in Philippines,
    35–36, 44, 46; the poor and, 46;
    Taiwan and, 30–31; World Bank vs.,
    35, 49
environmental crises: in China, 96–97;
    globalization and, 95; Washington
    Consensus and, 95–96
environmental degradation: aid and,
    48–49, 51; China and, 62; corporations
    and, 49; development and, 29, 30–31;
    equity and, 49; exports and, 61–62;
    free market and, 47–48; globalization
    and, 59, 61–62; Mexico and, 47–48,
    50, 61; in the North, 63; resources and,
    49, 51; the rich and, 45, 46, 47; in the
    South, 62; U.S. and, 47, 51
environmental issues: economic growth
    and, 2; Washington Consensus and, 3,
    27, 41
environmental myths, 41; about aid, 44,
    48–49; at Earth Summit (1992), 43,
    47, 49; about free market economic
    growth, 43–44, 46–48; Gore and, 44;
    about the poor, 42, 43, 44–46, 47;
    Washington Consensus and, 42
environmental projects, loans for, 51
environmental standards: corporate-led

globalization and, 64; corporations
    and, 65; free trade agreements and,
    64; NAFTA and, 65; Washington
    Consensus and, 75, 76
environmental sustainability: alter-
    globalization and, 103–104;
    citizen initiatives and, 36; Clinton
    administration and, 49; economic
    activity and, 47; economic growth and,
    36; Gore and, 47, 50; NICs and, 32; the
    poor and, 42, 51; socialist economies
    and, 32; structural adjustment and, 33,
    34; trade agreements and, 49, 50; U.S.
    and, 47
equity: citizen initiatives and, 35, 36;
    democracy and, 39; development
    and, 29; economic growth vs., 36,
    48; environmental degradation and,
    49; market mechanisms and, 32;
    resources and, 35–36, 48, 49; structural
    adjustment and, 33, 34. See also income
    inequalities
European Network on Debt and
    Development (EURODAD), 93, 121n3
European Union, 72, 101
exchange rates, competitive, 109n3
exports: developing countries and,
    16; East Asia (1970s) rapid, 14;
    environmental degradation and, 61–62;
    manufactured goods, 10; NICs and, 15,
    16, 19–20; poor nations raw material,
    10–11; protectionism and, 39; raw
    material, 10; the South and, 61–62;
    World Bank and, 63
Exxon Mobil, 3

fair trade, 63–64, 70, 101
Falk, Richard, 7, 110n8
Fallows, James, 110n13, 122n13
Far Eastern Economic Review, 17
Fay, Chip, 48
Federal Reserve, 3
financial crisis, 1997–1998 global. See East
    Asian crisis (1997)
financial liberalization, 109n3
fiscal discipline, 109n3
flat earth, of Friedman, Thomas, 82, 84
Focus on the Global South, 77

food: crisis (2008), 97; genetically
    engineered, 72
Ford Motor Company, 3, 59
Foreign Affairs, 74
Fortune 500 companies, 3
fossil fuels, 89, 97, 106
Fox, Jonathan, 118n8
free market: in 1970s, 14; 1980s failure of,
    29; 1980s misconceptions and, 29–30;
    anti—critics of, 74; Chile and, 12,
    13; Clinton administration and, 5, 55,
    59; development and, 2; development
    orthodoxy, 5–6; economic growth and,
    2; environmental degradation and, 47–
    48; environmental myths about, 43–44,
    46–48; export-led growth and, 3; false
    advertising of, 14; Friedman, Milton,
    and, 12, 13; fundamentalism, 5; Kenya
    and, 7, 12; labor and, 88; paradigm
    diminishing, 5; reformers of, 71–72;
    silent revolution, 13; ten consensus
    policy areas of, 109n3; terrorism
    and, 79, 82; ultra defenders of, 72;
    Washington Consensus and, 5. *See also*
    globalization; market fundamentalism;
    neoliberalism; Washington Consensus
free trade: Bush, George H. W., and, 44,
    49–50; Bush, George W., and, 79, 82;
    Friedman, Thomas, on, 89; middle
    class and, 56; rich/poor countries
    economic gap and, 56–57; U.S. and,
    56, 64, 79. *See also* North American
    Free Trade Agreement
free trade agreements: economic
    integration and, 64; environmental
    standards and, 64; labor rights and, 64
Free Trade Zone, 17
Friedman, Milton, 12; free market and, 13
Friedman, Thomas: alter-globalization
    and, 88, 89; Bush, George W.,
    administration and, 82; flat earth of,
    82, 84; on free trade, 89; on poverty,
    84, 85, 89; on protectionism, 89;
    Washington Consensus and, 80–81, 89
Friends of the Earth, 48, 77

G-8 summit (2005), 82
Gallagher, Kevin, 118n14, 122n10

General Agreement on Tariffs and Trade,
    20
genetically engineered food, 72
Germany, 14
Gills, Barry, 110n8
global backlash, 4; the poor and, 42, 81
global debt relief movement, 8
*Global Dreams: Imperial Corporations
    and the New World Order* (Barnet and
    Cavanagh), 59
global economy: in 1980s, 15; ever-
    changing, 7; post–World War II, 6
globalization: alternatives for, 99;
    from below, 4, 110n8; Clinton
    administration and, 59; environmental
    crises and, 95; environmental
    degradation and, 59, 61–62; income
    inequalities and, 59, 60, 85–86; job
    losses and, 59, 60–61; Mexico and,
    61; North-South, 59, 60, 119n5;
    poverty and, 84; protectionism and,
    89; U.S. and, 61; U.S. business and,
    59, 65; winners/losers of, 59. *See also*
    free market; market fundamentalism;
    neoliberalism; Washington Consensus
globalization alternatives: global,
    103–104; local, 100; national, 100–102;
    regional, 102–103
globalization, corporate-led:
    environmental standards and, 64; labor
    and, 64; NAFTA and, 54; the poor/
    rich and, 53–54; WTO and, 54
globalization movement: anti–, 4, 110n8;
    anti–corporate, 4. *See also* alter-
    globalization
global justice movement, 4
global lending institutions, 51
global North, 59, 62
global South, 59, 62, 77
Goldwater, Barry, 12
Gore, Al, 41, 42; Earth Summit (1992)
    and, 43; environmental myths and, 44;
    environmental sustainability and, 47, 50
government: development planning/
    policy role of, 10; interest groups
    and, 37; role in economy, 37. *See also*
    authoritarian governments
grants, aid as, 51

Great Depression (1930s), 11
Grossman, Gene, 46
Group of Eight, 75
Guatemala, 54

Haiti, 54
Hakim, Peter, 36
Hartmann, Betsy, 86
Heavily Indebted Poor Countries
    (HIPC), 74, 103, 118n9; alter-
    globalization and, 77
Helms, Jesse, 55
Hemispheric Social Alliance, 4
Heritage Foundation: IMF and, 72;
    Washington Consensus and, 13
HIPC. See Heavily Indebted Poor
    Countries
Hong Kong, 15, 18, 73
hot money, 70–71
human needs: citizen initiatives and, 36;
    economic growth vs., 36
human rights, citizen initiatives and, 36
hunger, neoliberalism and, 97
Huntington, Samuel, 39

IMF. See International Monetary Fund
import-substitution industrialization
    (ISI), 10–11; 1970s policies of, 13
income inequalities: globalization and, 59,
    60, 85–86; in the North, 63; rising, 86.
    See also equity
India, 4, 15, 35, 62; citizen organizations
    in, 38;; economic growth of, 96;
    poverty in, 83, 88; regulation in, 97
indigenous communities: development
    and, 1–2; environmental activism
    and, 35; in Philippines, 1–2, 6, 36,
    107; poverty of, 83–84; transnational
    agribusiness vs., 1–2; World Bank and,
    1–2, 4
Indonesia, 18, 62, 73
industrialization: authoritarian
    governments and, 39; import-
    substitution, 10
Industrial Promotion Policies in the Philippines
    (Power), 21
inequities. See equity
inflation, late–1970s hyper, 13

Institute for International Economics, 2
Institute for Policy Studies (IPS), 8
InterAmerican Development Bank, 7
interest groups, government and, 37
international commodity agreements:
    poor nations and, 11–12; U.S. and, 12
International Development Association, 94
International Forum on Globalization, 8,
    77, 82, 99, 103, 119n5
International Labor Organization (ILO), 64
International Monetary Fund (IMF):
    1980s austerity programs of, 23; 1982
    debt crisis and, 15, 24; 2007 changes at,
    94; Argentina and, 93; crises at, 92, 93,
    94, 95, 98, 121n3; developing countries
    and, 63, 73, 77; developing countries
    debt burden and, 63, 77; development
    and, 3, 7; East Asian crisis (1997) and,
    72, 92, 93; Heritage Foundation and,
    72; hot money and, 71; LDCs and, 16,
    112n5; neoliberalism and, 14; poor
    nations and, 94; reform of, 56, 72; the
    South and, 61; structural adjustment
    and, 32, 33, 34; universal development
    strategies of, 25; Washington Con-
    sensus and, 92; World Bank and, 73
investments: foreign direct, 109n3;
    North-South 1990s, 70–71; trade and,
    89. See also aid
IPS. See Institute for Policy Studies
Iran, 54
Iraq, 55

Japan: capitalist/socialist economies and,
    31; Washington Consensus and, 73
job losses: globalization and, 59, 60–61; in
    global North, 62
Jubilee debt cancellation, 103
Jubilee South debt cancellation network, 4

Kalaw, Maximo "Junie," 35–36
Keesing, Donald, 18
Kenya, free market and, 7, 12
Kerala. See India
Keynesian economics, 10
Keynes, John Maynard, 15; economics
    of, 10
Kissinger, Henry, 71

Klein, Naomi, 111n21
Kohl, Helmut, 14, 81
Kohli, Atul, 39Korea, 54
Korten, David, 114n19, 115n8, 122n15
Korten, Frances, 50, 51, 115n12
Kothari, Smitu, 118n8
Krueger, Alan, 46
Krugman, Paul, 71, 72
Kuznets curve, 60
Kuznets, Simon, 60
Kyoto Protocol, 104

labor: corporate-led globalization and,
    64; free market and, 88; structural
    adjustment and, 33–34
labor activism, 28; in South Korea, 29,
    30, 31
labor rights: free trade agreements and,
    64; in global North, 62; local markets
    and, 39; in Mexico, 61; NAFTA and,
    50, 64–65; trade agreements and,
    50; U.S. and, 64–65; Washington
    Consensus and, 75, 76
labor unions, 76
Lappe, Frances Moore, 123n15
Latin America, 4; in 1990s, 29; alter-
    globalization and, 80, 101, 105–106;
    citizen initiatives in, 36; opposition to
    neoliberalism, 80, 81, 96; U.S. and, 54,
    56; Washington Consensus and, 96
less developed countries (LDCs): IMF
    and, 16, 112n5; NICs and, 16; World
    Bank and, 16, 18, 112n5
Levi Strauss, 65
Lewis, W. Arthur, 7
Liberia, 107
Licaros, Gregorio, 17
Little Dragons, 14
loans: aid and, 50–51; developing
    countries and, 50–51; for
    environmental projects, 51; U.S. and,
    51; of World Bank, 51. See also aid
"lost decade" (1980s), 57
Lutzenberger, Jose, 48

Malawi, 94
Malaysia, 15, 73, 77
Mander, Jerry, 99, 123n16

Manila, 2
Marcos, Ferdinand, 1
market(s): big emerging, 64–65;
    common, 99; labor rights and local, 39;
    opening and protectionism, 89
market fundamentalism, 95, 98; era of,
    3, 8, 98; questions about, 9; of Soros,
    2. See also free market; globalization;
    neoliberalism; Washington Consensus
market mechanisms: command economics
    vs., 32; equity and, 32; mature
    economies and, 37–38
Marshall Plan, 48
McNamara, Robert, 4, 16, 71
media, Third World images of, 54–55
Mexico, 15, 42; 1994–1995 capital debacle
    of, 56; environmental degradation
    of, 47–48, 50, 61; globalization and,
    61; labor rights in, 61; opposition to
    neoliberalism, 96; U.S. and, 43, 50, 56
middle class, free trade and, 56
Milanovic, Branko, 120n20
Mittelman, James, 110n8
modernization: development and, 84–86,
    109n1; poverty and, 84–86
Multi-Fiber Arrangement, 20
Multilateral Agreement on Investment
    (MAI), 70, 76

Nader, Ralph, 76
NAFTA. See North American Free Trade
    Agreement
neoconservatives, 93
neoliberalism: alternatives to, 8, 81;
    backlash against, 5, 80; Brazil and, 98;
    citizen organizations and, 81; Clinton
    administration and, 42; critiques of, 5,
    8; debates over, 9; history of, 5, 7, 15;
    hunger and, 97; IMF and, 14; Latin
    American opposition to, 80, 81, 96;
    Mexico opposition to, 96; poverty and,
    97; protests against, 8; questions about,
    9; rise of, 15; ten consensus policy areas
    of, 109n3; Washington Consensus
    as, 2, 3; World Bank and, 14. See also
    free market; globalization; market
    fundamentalism; Washington Consensus
Netherlands, 52

New International Economic Order
(1970s), 11, 99
Newly Industrializing Countries (NICs),
14; Asian, 18–19, 26, 30; Clinton
administration and, 53; competition
between, 17–22; developing countries
and, 32; environmental sustainability
and, 32; exports and, 15, 16, 19–20;
LDCs and, 16; political participation
and, 32; slow growth (1970s/1980s)
and, 19–20, 21–22; socialist economies
vs., 31, 32; World Bank and, 15–17,
18; would-be NICs and, 19. See also
developing countries; poor nations;
Third World
New York Times, 82, 92
Nicaragua, 11, 54, 96
NICs. See Newly Industrializing
Countries
Nixon, Richard, 10
the North: environmental degradation in,
63; global, 59, 62; income inequalities
in, 63; resource flow to, 63. See also
North-South; the South; Third World
North American Free Trade Agreement
(NAFTA): Bush, George H. W., and,
49–50; citizen backlash to, 43; Clinton
administration and, 42, 43, 49, 50,
55, 56; corporate-led globalization
and, 54; development debate and, 43;
environmental standards and, 65; labor
rights and, 50, 64–65; Washington
Consensus and, 42
North Korea, 55
North-South: in 1990s, 62; 1990s
investments, 70–71; framework, 53;
globalization, 59, 60, 119n5; policy
agenda, 55, 56. See also the North; the
South; Third World
North-South gap: 1982 debt crisis and,
57–58; 1990s widening of, 59, 62;
bottom 45 percent and, 64; Clinton
administration and, 62; enlightened self-
interest toward, 65–66; WTO and, 95
Nyerere, Julius, 7

oil. See fossil fuels
Olivera, Oscar, 100

Organization of Petroleum Exporting
Countries (OPEC), 11

Paraguay, 96
People's Agrarian Reform Code, 36–37
people's organizations. See citizen
initiatives
People's Republic of China (PRC). See
China
Philippines, 19, 36; citizen organizations
of, 36–37, 101; Consensus backlash
of, 4; development debate in, 7; early
neoliberalism in, 6; environmental
activism in, 35–36, 44, 46; indigenous
communities in, 1–2, 6, 36, 107;
interest groups in, 37; SALs and, 16–17;
southern development of, 1–2, 6; U.S.
and, 51–52; Washington Consensus
and, 7; World Bank and, 4, 7, 16–17,
18, 21
Pinochet, Augusto, 12
political issues: economic growth and, 2;
Washington Consensus and, 3
political participation: citizen initiatives
and, 35, 36; citizen organizations and,
37; development and, 29; economic
growth vs., 36; NICs and, 32;
socialist economies and, 32; structural
adjustment and, 33, 34; sustainable
development and, 37, 39
the poor: corporate-led globalization and,
53–54; environmental activism and,
46; environmental myths about, 42, 43,
44–46, 47; environmental sustainability
and, 42, 51; global backlash and, 42,
81; rural, 83–84; U.S. and, 63. See also
equity; income inequalities; poverty
poor nations: 1982 debt crisis and, 14, 15,
57; economic gap with rich nations,
56–57; global economic architecture
of, 11; IMF and, 94; international
commodity agreements and, 11–12;
OPEC and, 11; raw material exports
of, 10–11; rich vs., 11–12; Washington
Consensus and, 94; World Bank and,
94. See also developing countries;
Newly Industrializing Countries; the
South; Third World

poverty: in Africa, 83, 86–87, 88; aid and, 86–87; causes of, 84–85; in China, 83, 88; deceptive measuring of, 83; in development debate, 85; extreme, 83; Friedman, Thomas, on, 84, 85, 89; globalization and, 84; in India, 83, 88; of indigenous communities, 83–84; modernization and, 84–86; neoliberalism and, 97; regulation and, 88; Sachs, Jeffrey, on, 82, 83, 84–85, 86, 87, 89; in the South, 62; terrorism and, 79, 82; trade and, 87–88; U.S. and, 85; Washington Consensus and, 80–81, 82, 83–84. See also the poor
Power, John, 21
Prebisch, Raul, 10, 11, 15
privatization, 81; of state-owned firms, 3; in Washington Consensus economic-reform areas, 109n3
The Progress of Policy Reform in Latin America (Williamson), 109n3
property rights, 109n3
protectionism: exports and, 39; Friedman, Thomas, on, 89; globalization and, 89; market opening and, 89; new, 20; World Bank and, 20–21
Public Citizen, 76
public expenditure priorities, 109n3

raw material exports, 10
Reagan, Ronald, 7, 14, 81
regulation, 75; in China, 97; in India, 97; poverty and, 88
Reich, Robert, 98
Report and Recommendation (August 1980), 21
Republican party, 61
resources: democratization of, 51; environmental degradation and, 49, 51; equity and, 35–36, 48, 49; flow to North, 63; trade exploitation of, 65
the rich: corporate-led globalization and, 53–54; environmental degradation and, 45, 46, 47. See also equity; income inequalities
rich nations: economic gap with poor nations, 56–57; poor vs., 11–12
Rodrik, Dani, 88
Roosevelt, Franklin, 64

Rostow, Walt Whitman, 86
Rubin, Robert, 71
Rwanda, 54
"the Rwanda image," 54

Sachs, Jeffrey, 72; on aid, 86, 87, 89; alter-globalization and, 88, 89; Bush, George W., administration and, 82; on poverty, 82, 83, 84–85, 86, 87, 89; Washington Consensus and, 80–81, 82, 83, 89
Sachs, Wolfgang, 109n1
SALs. See structural adjustment loans
Scholte, Jan Aart, 110n8
Sears, 65
Seattle Coalition, 8; WTO and, 28, 67, 68, 76, 81
September 11, 2001: Bush, George W., and, 82, 98; Washington Consensus and, 8, 9, 79, 82, 98
Shiva, Vandana, 46, 85
Shultz, George, 72
silent revolution, 36
Simon, William E., 72
Singapore, 15, 18
slow growth (late 1970s/early 1980s): NICs and, 19–20, 21–22; World Bank and, 19–20, 21–22
Smith, Jackie, 110n9
social issues: economic growth and, 2; Washington Consensus and, 3
socialist economies: capitalist economies vs., 31; development and, 30, 31; of Eastern Europe, 30, 31, 32; environmental sustainability and, 32; Japan and, 31; NICs vs., 31, 32; political participation and, 32
social movements, 100
Somalia, 54
Soros, George, 2, 109n2
the South: bottom 45 percent and, 63; Clinton administration and, 55, 56; environmental degradation in, 62; exports and, 61–62; global, 59, 62, 77; global North in, 62; IMF and, 61; poverty in, 62; U.S. and, 55, 56; World Bank and, 61. See also North-South; the North; Third World

South Africa, 36
Southeast Asia Chronicle, 18
South Korea, 14, 15, 18; in 1990s, 29–30, 31–32, 37, 39, 40; authoritarian government of, 39; command economics of, 31–32; labor activism in, 29, 30, 31
Soviet Union, 40, 55
Sri Lanka, 17, 18, 19
The Stages of Economic Growth: A Non-Communist Manifesto (Rostow), 86
stagnation, World Bank and global, 22
Stiglitz, Joseph, 71, 75, 118n12, 118n13
Strauss-Kahn, Dominique, 94
Stremlau, John, 56
Strong, Maurice, 48
structural adjustment, 16, 30; developing countries and, 32; environmental sustainability and, 33, 34; equity and, 33, 34; failure of, 33–34; IMF and, 32, 33, 34; labor and, 33–34; political participation and, 33, 34; World Bank and, 32, 33, 34
structural adjustment loans (SALs): Philippines and, 16–17; of World Bank, 9, 16–17
structural inequities, Washington Consensus and, 27
structuralist, 10
subsidiarity, 123n16
suffering, development and, 29
Summers, Lawrence, 44, 47, 71, 74, 75
sustainable development: authoritarian governments and, 39; citizen initiatives and, 38; citizen organizations and, 36, 38–39; democracy and, 39; political participation and, 37, 39; U.S. and, 52; World Bank and, 51. *See also* development

Taiwan, 14, 15, 18; in 1990s, 29, 30–31; authoritarian government of, 39; environmental activism and, 30–31
Tanzania, self-reliant path of, 7, 11, 99
tariffs, economic growth and, 88
tax reform, 109n3
technologies, new, 19
terrorism: Bush, George W.,

administration and, 98; free market and, 79, 82; poverty and, 79, 82
Thailand, 15, 18, 101
Thatcher, Margaret, 14, 81
think tanks, 3
Third World: 1982 debt crisis and, 23; Clinton administration and, 54–55; Clinton administration images of, 54–55, 56; debt of, 7, 23; media images of, 54–55. *See also* developing countries; Newly Industrializing Countries; poor nations; the North; the South
Third World Network, 77
Tickner, Ann, 110n13
TNCS. *See* transnational corporations
Tobin, James, 77
Tobin tax, 77
trade: in 21st century, 81; aid and, 87–88; declining terms of, 10; economic growth and, 87, 88; investments and, 89; poverty and, 87–88; resource exploitation of, 65. *See also* fair trade; free trade
trade agreements: cooperative, 11; environmental sustainability and, 49, 50; labor rights and, 50; labor rights in, 50
trade blocs, regional, 11
trade liberalization, 3; in Washington Consensus economic-reform areas, 109n3
transnational agribusiness, *vs.* indigenous communities, 1–2
transnational corporations (TNCS), 17
Truman, Harry, 6; 1949 U.S. program of development of, 109n1
Turkey, 93

UN. *See* United Nations
UNCTAD. *See* United Nations Conference on Trade and Development
United Nations (UN): development debate in, 7; Millennium Development Goals, 83
United Nations Children's Fund, 29
United Nations Conference on Environment and Development, 41
United Nations Conference on Trade and

Development (UNCTAD): 1984, 31; developing countries and, 16; pre-Consensus era of, 6–7, 11
United Nations Covenant on Economic, Social and Cultural Rights, 36
United Nations Development Program, 82, 101
United Nations Earth Summit. *See* Earth Summit (1992)
United States (U.S.): 1949 program of development of, 109n1; 1982 debt crisis and, 24; Africa and, 54; aid and, 63; Asia and, 54; bottom 45 percent and, 63; developing countries and, 53; environmental degradation and, 47, 51; environmental sustainability and, 47; free trade and, 56, 64, 79; globalization and, 61; international commodity agreements and, 12; labor rights and, 64–65; Latin America and, 54, 56; loans and, 51; Mexico and, 43, 50, 56; Philippines and, 51–52; the poor and, 63; poverty and, 85; the South and, 55, 56; sustainable development and, 52; Washington Consensus and, 3, 14, 74; World Bank and, 93; WTO and, 79
Uruguay, 96
U.S. Agency for International Development, 48, 49
U.S. bilateral lending agency, 51
U.S. business, globalization and, 59, 65
U.S. Commerce Department, 56
U.S. Congress, 7; Clinton administration and Republican, 55, 56
U.S. Treasury Department, 7, 74, 75

Vandermoortele, Jan, 119n6, 119n7, 120n21, 120n32
Venezuela, 81, 92, 96, 101
Vietnam, 32, 54

Wade, Robert Hunter, 118n14, 121n36, 121n37, 122n10
Wall Street, 74, 75
Wal-Mart, 3, 59; economy and alter-globalization, 88
Washington Consensus: 1990s expansion of, 27; alter-globalization and, 4, 8,
80, 89, 91, 110n8; alternatives to, 99–104; backlash against, 3–4, 8, 72; Berlin Wall fall and, 28; Clinton administration and, 53; crack (late 90's) in, 67–78, 79; debates over, 9, 72; developing countries and, 33, 73, 91; economic growth and, 27, 68, 80; economic reform and, 3; elite dissent toward, 71–74, 80; emergence of, 13–26; environmental crises and, 95–96; environmental issues and, 3, 27, 41; environmental myths and, 42; environmental standards and, 75, 76; era pre-, 6–7; European questioning of, 72; fact *vs.* theory in, 3; flaws of, 9; free market and, 5; Friedman, Thomas, and, 80–81, 89; Heritage Foundation and, 13; history of, 5, 8, 13–26, 27, 91; IMF and, 92; Japan and, 73; labor rights and, 75, 76; Latin America and, 96; myths of, 9, 79, 82–90; NAFTA and, 42; neoliberalism as, 2, 3; Philippines and, 7; political issues and, 3; poor nations and, 94; popular participation bypassing of, 27; post-, 75, 104; poverty and, 80–81, 82, 83–84; present and future of, 92; present day defenders of, 98; questions about, 9; rise and fall of, 5, 107; Sachs, Jeffrey, and, 80–81, 82, 83, 89; September 11, 2001, and, 8, 9, 79, 82, 98; social issues and, 3; structural inequities and, 27; ten reform areas of, 3, 109n3; U.S. and, 3, 14, 74; of Williamson, 2–3, 95, 109n3; World Bank and, 75, 92, 93; WTO and, 92. *See also* free market; globalization; market fundamentalism; neoliberalism
Washington of the 1980s, 3
Weisbrot, Mark, 88, 111n20, 121n36, 122n5
Williamson, John, 2–3, 95, 109n3
Wise, Timothy, 118n14, 122n10
Wisner, Ben, 87
Wolfensohn, James, 73, 117n8
Wolfowitz, Paul, 93
workers' rights. *See* labor rights
Workshop on International Regulations, 103

World Bank, 107; 1970s/1980s slow
  growth and, 19–20, 21–22; 1982 debt
  crisis and, 15, 23, 24; 2007 changes at,
  94; Bush, George W., administration
  and, 93, 94; crises at, 92, 93, 94, 95,
  98; developing countries debt burden
  and, 63; development and, 3, 7;
  doubtful research/proclamations of,
  93, 122n4; environmental activism
  vs., 35, 49; exports and, 63; global
  stagnation and, 22; IMF and, 73;
  indigenous communities and, 1–2, 4;
  LDCs and, 16, 18, 112n5; loans of, 51;
  neoliberalism and, 14; NICs and, 15–17,
  18; Philippines and, 4, 7, 16–17, 18, 21;
  poor nations and, 94; protectionism and,
  20–21; reform of, 56, 73–74, 117n8;
  resistance to, 4; SALs of, 9, 16–17; the
  South and, 61; structural adjustment
  and, 32, 33, 34; sustainable development
  and, 51; universal development strategies
  of, 25; U.S. and, 93; Washington
  Consensus and, 75, 92, 93

World Development Report (1978), 21–22
World Economic Survey 1987, 26
World Health Organization, 7
The World Is Flat (Friedman, Thomas),
  80, 81
World Social Forum, 4
World Trade Organization (WTO), 50;
  citizen organizations and, 76; Clinton
  administration and, 56; corporate-led
  globalization and, 54; crises at, 92, 95,
  98; North-South gap and, 95; Seattle
  Coalition and, 28, 67, 68, 76, 81; U.S.
  and, 79; Washington Consensus and,
  92
World War II: development debate post–,
  10; global economy post–, 6
WorldWatch Institute, 35
Wriston, Walter, 72
WTO. *See* World Trade Organization
  (WTO)

Zoellick, Robert, 94

About the Authors

Robin Broad is Professor of International Development at the School of International Service at American University. John Cavanagh directs the Institute for Policy Studies and is board chair of the International Forum on Globalization. This husband and wife team traveled from Geneva to the rural Philippines to Washington, D.C., to write this book, as well as their award-winning *Plundering Paradise: The Struggle for the Environment in the Philippines.*

Broad and Cavanagh have been writing together since they met as graduate students at Princeton University in the late 1970s.

This book builds on their range of experiences over the last thirty years—from the United Nations in Geneva (John) to the U.S. Treasury Department (Robin), to the "Battle of Seattle" where John debated corporate and government leaders, to the World Social Forum.

They have lived and worked in the Philippines several years, including a year they spent under a grant from the John D. and Catherine T. MacArthur Foundation.

Their experience in global institutions and the U.S. government and their years working with poorer communities give them unique insights into the impacts of global rules and institutions on ordinary people around the world.

Widely published (from the *New York Times* and *Washington Post* to *Foreign Policy* and top academic journals), they are known for their ability to combine political-economic analysis with accessible prose, making their work of interest to academics and lay persons.

Broad and Cavanagh live outside of Washington, D.C., with their eleven-year-old son, Jesse.